The Snark Handbook

POLITICS & GOVERNMENT EDITION

Also by Lawrence Dorfman

The Snark Handbook:
A Reference Guide to Verbal Sparring

The Snark Handbook: Insult Edition:
Comebacks, Taunts, Retorts, and Affronteries

The Snark Handbook: Sex Edition:
Innuendo, Irony, and Ill–Advised Insults on Intimacy

Snark! The Herald Angels Sing:
Sarcasm, Bitterness, and the Holiday Season

The Cigar Lover's Compendium

The Snark Handbook

POLITICS & GOVERNMENT EDITION

GRIDLOCK, RED TAPE, AND OTHER INSULTS TO WE THE PEOPLE

LAWRENCE DORFMAN

Skyhorse Publishing

Skyhorse Publishing books may be purchased in bulk at special discounts for sales promotion, corporate gifts, fund-raising, or educational purposes. Special editions can also be created to specifications. For details, contact the Special Sales Department, Skyhorse Publishing, 307 West 36th Street, 11th Floor, New York, NY 10018 or info@skyhorsepublishing.com.

Skyhorse® and Skyhorse Publishing® are registered trademarks of Skyhorse Publishing, Inc.®, a Delaware corporation.

Visit our website at www.skyhorsepublishing.com.

10 9 8 7 6 5 4 3 2 1

Library of Congress Cataloging-in-Publication Data is available on file.

ISBN: 978-1-61608-735-7

Printed in China

I believe there is something out there, watching us.
Unfortunately, it's the government.
—WOODY ALLEN

Politics, n. A strife of interests masquerading as a contest of principles. The conduct of public affairs for private advantage.

CONTENTS

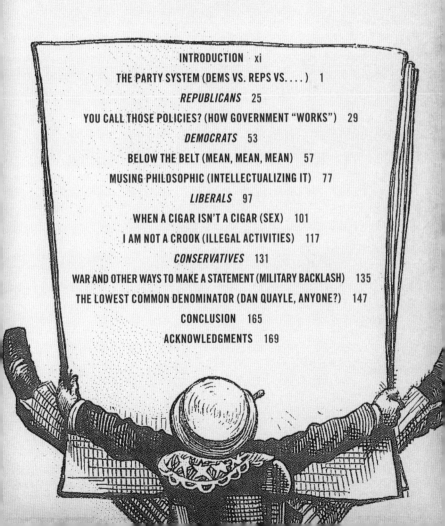

The Snark Handbook

POLITICS & GOVERNMENT EDITION

We hold these truths to be self-evident, that all men are created equal, that they are en-

Introduction

Congress: these, for the most part, illiterate hacks whose
fancy vests are spotted with gravy and whose speeches,
hypocritical, unctuous, and slovenly, are spotted also with
the gravy of political patronage.
—MARY MCCARTHY

HERE'S A FUN LITTLE experiment . . . pony up
to any bar in America, order a beer, and ask the
guy or gal next to you about politics or the government. Almost without fail, you'll hear one or more of these sentences
as part of the collective diatribe:

"I hate politics!"

"For the amount of money that WE pay those guys,
you'd think they could do something that would help the
average person."

"No matter who is in office, he screws it up."

"Why bother? What difference does it make?"

A line from the movie *Body Heat* sums it all up rather
nicely: "Sometimes the shit comes down so heavy I feel like

I should wear a hat." As far as I'm concerned, it's gotten so thick in the last thirty years, that there's not a hat big enough, wide enough, or strong enough to withstand the deluge we're being hit with every single day.

But what's worse? The politicians themselves—bloated, self-righteous, morally superior, condescending—or the way the Press (Capital P), those who actually cover politics, spend so little time letting us know what the candidate's positions are and spend most of their efforts focused on (or sometimes even spurring on) the backbiting, infighting, nasty clawing that Politics (Capital P) have become. (See answer, below).[1]

"But Mr. Snark," you might wonder, "Aren't all things nasty your bailiwick, your forte, your wheelhouse?" Well yes, sorta . . . but the kind of vitriolic back and forth I'm talking about is manufactured to disconnect us from the issues and focus our attentions on the banal muck of the moment.

Politics today have ceased to be about smart leadership and forward thinking. Talk to your bar buddy again—the foremost perception out there is that politicians will say or do anything to get into office. Sometimes they get caught, trying to be all things to all people. The "Cult of Personality" that Living Color sang about has certainly infected politics. Policy is now on a par with personal. Which candidate had an affair with what secretary? Whose tax return from twenty years ago might not be quite on the up and up? What was the

---

[1]   Trick question: They are both sides of the same coin.

and the pursuit of happiness. That to secure these rights, governments are instituted

name of that intern? He claims to have invented what? His family did what?

It goes on and on and on and on and . . . well, you know the rest.

Long ago and far away, on a planet much like our own, politicians needed to have certain qualities that the American public felt was their inalienable right to expect. The buzz-words of the day that were used to portray candidates were mostly positive: forthright . . . honest . . . focused . . . strong leadership . . . frank . . . direct.

Today, the headlines and the pundits bandy about words like ambitious . . . manipulative . . . deceptive . . . devious . . .

And that's the way they describe the good ones.

Which is not to say that everyone in the past was that upstanding. Throughout the history of the United States of America, there have always been those that sought the refuge of Snark. And rightly so.

Even George Washington[2] was known to be the butt of a few strategically placed barbs. In those days, they didn't spend so much time on appearance ("Are those his real eyebrows? Are those her real . . . whatevers?"). They actually passed judgment on each other's actions. What a concept. By 1827, most of the political writers of the day were pretty

---

[2]   Who, incidentally, is the only president not to blame the previous administration for his troubles.

among men, deriving their just powers from the consent of the governed. That whenever

well versed in throwing around well-aimed snark. Check this one out:

> I like the smell of a dunged field, and the tumult of a
> popular election.
> —AUGUSTUS WILLIAM HARE

Makes its point, no?

Sarcasm and snide remarks don't usually play well in a political campaign . . . and naturally snarky politicos have traditionally avoided it in their public speeches. But as you'll see in these pages, the Art of the Snark has its roots in ancient politics. Yes, my friends, if you burrow through the rhetoric and misleading propaganda, you'll find snark, and plenty of it.

But don't despair. Americans are known to be optimistic, to keep waiting for the light at the end of the tunnel.

Let's just hope that light is not an oncoming train.

o alter or to abolish it, and to institute new government, laying its foundation on such

principles and organizing its powers in such form, as to them shall seem most likely to

The Party System

It makes no difference which one you vote for—
the two parties are really one party representing
four percent of the people.
—GORE VIDAL

IN 1965, THE POP singer Lesley Gore had a hit record with a song that, taken in another context, can be construed to be just as relevant and as poignant today ... "It's my party and I'll cry if I want to." Sometimes, it amazing we're not all weeping openly at every turn.

It's tiring, this thing we call politics. Nowadays, the campaign trail begins immediately after the last election and ends ... well ... it pretty much never ends.

And why does everyone always have to pick a team? Are you a Democrat? A Republican? An old-school Republican, which is apparently the same thing as a conservative Democrat? And forget about that whole "third party" thing ...

ffect their safety and happiness. Prudence, indeed, will dictate that governments long

We are constantly being inundated from every angle—with ads, speeches, and debates—online through emails and political Emags—The Daily Beast, Politico, The Drudge Report, and The Huffington Post—on TV, from the Daily Show to The Colbert Report to Meet The Press to GMA. No respite in the movies either . . . seems like George Clooney has it in his contract that he gets to do a political thriller every four years, no matter what.

Yes, it's my party and I'll cry 'cos I HAVE to.

Please, somebody . . . make it stop?? Please?

When it comes to facing up to serious problems, each candidate will pledge to appoint a committee. And what is a committee? A group of the unwilling, picked from the unfit, to do the unnecessary. But it all sounds great in a campaign speech.
—RICHARD LONG HARKNESS

I honestly believe there are people so excited over this election that they must think that the President has something to do with running this country.
—WILL ROGERS

++

Why pay money to have your family tree traced; go into politics and your opponents will do it for you.
—ANON

+++

Democracy is also a form of worship. It is the worship of Jackals by Jackasses.
—HENRY LOUIS MENCKEN

~♦~

Every election, one candidate accuses another of being a "lifelong politician" or a "Washington insider." That just cuts to the quick . . . guess the former really is wild and untamed. A maverick, perhaps. But tell me, when did knowing how the government works become a bad thing?

~♦~

If the person you are trying to diagnose politically is some sort of intellectual, the chances are two to one he is a Democrat.
—VANCE PACKARD

♦♦

I might be in favor of national healthcare if it required all Democrats to get their heads examined.
—ANN COULTER

♦♦♦

xperience hath shown that mankind are more disposed to suffer, while evils are suf-

And on the seventh day, God stepped back and said, "This is my creation, perfect in every way . . . oh, dammit I left all this pot all over the place. Now they'll think I want them to smoke it . . . Now I have to create Republicans.

—BILL HICKS

♦♦

You've got the brainwashed, that's the Democrats, and the brain-dead, that's the Republicans.

—MARK RUSSELL

~♦~

When two candidates in the same party are running neck and neck, it's often suggested that one serve as the other's ticket mate if he fails to win the GOP nomination for President. That's some plan . . . history tells us that the best way to never hear from a candidate again is to make him Vice President.

~♦~

In my lifetime, we've gone from Eisenhower to George W. Bush. We've gone from John F. Kennedy to Al Gore. If this is evolution, I believe that in twelve years, we'll be voting for plants.

—LEWIS BLACK

♦♦♦

ferable, than to right themselves by abolishing the forms to which they are accustomed

Women are now being considered as candidates for the Vice Presidency because it is the worst job in America. A job with real power is the First Lady. I'd be willing to run for that. As far as the men who are running for President are concerned, they aren't even people I would date.

—NORA EPHRON

++

We have a two-party system. One party wins the election and the other tells us about the mistake we've made for the next four years.

—TOMMY KOENIG

+++

In this world of sin and sorrow there is always something to be thankful for; as for me, I rejoice that I am not a Republican.

—H. L. MENCKEN

++

A Democrat sees the glass of water as half full. A Republican looks at the same glass, and wonders who the hell drank his water.

—JEFF CESARIO

+++

Politicians are the same the world over. They promise to build a bridge even when there's no river.

—NIKITA KRUSCHEV

++

Ninety-eight percent of the adults in this country are decent, hard-working, honest Americans. It's the other two percent that get all the publicity. But then—we elected them.

—LILY TOMLIN

~•~

A woman in a hot air balloon realized she was lost. She lowered her altitude and spotted a man in a boat below. She shouted to him, "Excuse me, can you help me? I promised a friend I would meet him an hour ago, but I don't know where I am."

The man consulted his portable GPS and replied, "You're in a hot air balloon, approximately 30 feet above ground elevation of 2,346 feet above sea level. You are at 31 degrees, 14.97 minutes north latitude and 100 degrees, 49.09 minutes west longitude."

She rolled her eyes and said, "You must be a Democrat."

"I am," replied the man. "How did you know?"

"Well," answered the balloonist, "everything you told me is technically correct. But I have no idea what to do with your information, and I'm

evinces a design to reduce them under absolute despotism, it is their right, it is the

still lost. Frankly, you've not been much help to me."

The man smiled and responded, "You must be a Republican."

"I am," replied the balloonist. "How did you know?"

"Well," said the man, "you don't know where you are or where you are going. You've risen to where you are due to a large quantity of hot air. You made a promise you have no idea how to keep, and you expect me to solve your problem. You're in exactly the same position you were in before we met, but somehow, now it's my fault."

~•~

Giving money and power to government is like giving whiskey and car keys to teenage boys.
—P. J. O'ROURKE

♦♦♦

He knows nothing and thinks he knows everything. That points clearly to a political career.
—GEORGE BERNARD SHAW

♦♦

Public office is the last refuge of the incompetent.
—BOISE PENROSE

♦♦♦

duty, to throw off such government, and to provide new guards for their future security.

Obama achieved the same kind of compromise with the Republicans that Custer reached with Sitting Bull.
—DAVID LETTERMAN

••

Barack Obama recently said that politics has become too gummed up by money and influence . . . and then he had to leave to attend a fundraiser.
—JAY LENO

•••

Clinton left the White House with all the class of an XFL halftime show.
—BILL MAHER

••

Reagan won because he ran against Jimmy Carter. Had he run unopposed he would have lost.
—MORT SAHL

•••

Patriotism is your conviction that this country is superior to all others because you were born in it.
—GEORGE BERNARD SHAW

••

Popularity, I have always thought, may aptly be compared to a coquette—the more you woo her, the more apt is she to elude your embrace.
—JOHN TYLER

•••

Donkey vs. Elephant[3]

A. Bob Hope
[on Lyndon Johnson]
B. H. L. Mencken
[on Franklin D. Roosevelt]
C. Clarence Darrow
[on J. Edgar Hoover]

D. Theodore Roosevelt
[on Woodrow Wilson]
E. U.S. Grant
[on James Garfield]
F. Harry Truman
[on Franklin Pierce]

~+~

1. If elected, he will do one thing that is almost incomprehensible to the human mind; he will make a great man out of Coolidge.
2. You can tell he used to be a rancher—he squeezes Republicans like he's milking cows.
3. He is not possessed of the backbone of an angleworm.
4. If he became convinced tomorrow that coming out for cannibalism would get him votes he needs, he would begin fattening a missionary in the White House backyard.
5. A complete fizzle . . . he didn't know what was going on, and even if he had, he wouldn't have known what to do about it.
6. An infernal skunk in the White House.

---

[3]   1.C., 2.A., 3.E., 4.B., 5.F., 6.D.

which constrains them to alter their former systems of government. The history of the

In our two party system, the Democrats are the party of no ideas and the Republicans the party of bad ideas.
—LEWIS BLACK

+++

The future historian, if free from prejudice and plutocratic influence, will stamp William McKinley as the pliant tool of trusts and monopolists.
—ANON

++

The Democrats seem to be basically nicer people, but they have demonstrated time and again that they have the management skills of celery. They're the kind of people who'd stop to help you change a flat, but would somehow manage to set your car on fire. I would be reluctant to entrust them with a Cuisinart, let alone the economy. The Republicans, on the other hand, would know how to fix your tire, but they wouldn't bother to stop because they'd want to be on time for Ugly Pants Night at the country club.
—DAVE BARRY

+++

The only difference between death and taxes is that death doesn't get worse every time Congress meets.
—WILL ROGERS

++

present King of Great Britain is a history of repeated injuries and usurpations, all hav

~✦~

President Clinton, speaking in private with his advisor on public favor, told him that the planned invasion of Haiti will be the most unpopular thing that he has ever done as the President of the United States.

"Actually, sir, according to our research, the most unpopular thing you've ever done was to be inaugurated as President. It's just been downhill from there."

~✦~

If the Republicans will stop telling lies about the Democrats, we will stop telling the truth about them.

—ADLAI STEVENSON

✦✦✦

I wish we lived in a place more like the America of yesteryear that only exists in the brains of us Republicans.

—NED FLANDERS

✦✦

The Republican convention started this past weekend, so don't forget to turn your clocks back four hundred years.

—JAY LENO

✦✦✦

ing in direct object the establishment of an absolute tyranny over these states. To prove

The outcome of twenty-five years of Republican rule is that Americans have learned to hate themselves, like children of repressive, conformist families.

—CYNTHIA HEIMEL

✦✦

I like Republicans, and would trust them with anything in the world except public office.

—ADLAI STEVENSON

✦✦✦

Why do Republicans hate gay marriage so much? They certainly don't hate gay prostitutes.

—MARGARET CHO

~✦~

When told by an aide that Wendell Wilkie had his eye on the President's chair, FDR replied, "Ah yes, but look what I've got on it."

~✦~

My grandmother's brain was dead, but her heart was still beating. It was the first time we ever had a Democrat in the family.

—EMO PHILIPS

✦✦

this, let facts be submitted to a candid world. ✦ He has refused his assent to laws, the

~✦~

They say that Christopher Columbus was the first Democrat. When he left to discover America, he didn't know where he was going. When he got there he didn't know where he was. And it was all done on a government grant.

~✦~

Democrats can't get elected unless things get worse—and things won't get worse unless they get elected.
—JEANE KIRKPATRICK

✦✦✦

One of the many problems with the American left, and indeed of the American left, has been its image and self-image as something rather too solemn, mirthless, herbivorous, dull, monochrome, righteous, and boring.
—CHRISTOPHER HITCHENS

✦✦

A Liberal is someone who feels a great debt to his fellow man, which debt he proposes to pay off with your money.
—G. GORDON LIDDY

✦✦✦

What the Liberal really wants is to bring about change that
will not in any way endanger his position.

—STOKELY CARMICHAEL

++

Liberals love America like O.J. loved Nicole.

—ANN COULTER

+++

As usual the Liberals offer a mixture of sound and original
ideas. Unfortunately none of the sound ideas are original
and none of the original ideas are sound.

—HAROLD MACMILLAN

++

Conservative, n: A statesman who is enamored of existing
evils, as distinguished from the Liberal who wishes to
replace them with others.

—AMBROSE BIERCE

+++

A conservative is a man with two perfectly good legs who,
however, has never learned how to walk forward.

—FRANKLIN D. ROOSEVELT

++

My kid is a conservative. Why is that? Remember in the 60s,
when we told you if you kept doing drugs your kids would be
mutants?

—MORT SAHL

+++

to pass laws of immediate and pressing importance, unless suspended in their operation

Our 'neoconservatives' are neither new nor conservative, but
old as Babylon and evil as Hell.
—EDWARD ABBEY

✦✦

Conservatives are not necessarily stupid, but most stupid
people are conservatives.
—JOHN STUART MILL

✦✦✦

During an election campaign, the air is full of speeches and
vice versa.
—HENRY ADAMS

✦✦

Our politicians are a bunch of yo-yos. The presidency is
now a cross between a popularity contest and a high school
debate, with an encyclopedia of clichés as the first prize.
—SAUL BELLOW

✦✦✦

Bad officials are elected by good citizens who do not vote.
—GEORGE JEAN NATHAN

✦✦

If voting changed anything, they'd make it illegal.
Vote for the man who promises least; he'll be the least
disappointing.
—BERNARD BARUCH

✦✦✦

ll his assent should be obtained; and when so suspended, he has utterly neglected to

Don't vote for politicians. It just encourages them.
—BILLY CONNOLLY

✦✦

TOP POLITICAL SLOGANS

1. Reagan—"Are you better off than you were four years ago?"—Huh. And what's the definition of "better off?"
2. Obama—"Yes We Can!"—Well, clearly, no, we can't . . . or better yet, "No, We Don't Wanna."
3. Perot—"Ross For Boss"—What the hell were they thinking?
4. Nixon—"Nixon's The One"—As in, "One, two, test, test . . . is this thing on?"
5. Hoover—"A chicken in every pot and a car in every garage"—the granddaddy of 'em all. Today, no one can afford chicken and there's pot in every garage.
6. Harrison—"Tippecanoe and Tyler Too"—No new ideas? Rhyme something.
7. Eisenhower—"I Like Ike"—see above.

It's dangerous for a national candidate to say things that people might remember.
—EUGENE MCCARTHY

✦✦

attend to them. ✦ He has refused to pass other laws for the accommodation of large dis

If you think too much about getting re-elected, it is very difficult to be worth re-electing.
—WOODROW WILSON

✦✦✦

My esteem in this country has gone up substantially. It is much nicer now that when people wave at me, they use all their fingers.
—JIMMY CARTER

✦✦

I was America's first instant Vice President—and now, America's first instant President. The Marine Corps Band was so confused, they didn't know whether to play 'Hail to the Chief' or 'You've Come a Long Way, Baby.'
—GERALD FORD

✦✦✦

The mistake a lot of politicians make is forgetting they've been appointed and thinking they've been anointed.
—CLAUDE PEPPER

✦✦

Congress is so strange. A man gets up to speak and says nothing. Nobody listens—and then everybody disagrees.
—BORIS MARSHALOV

✦✦✦

icts of people, unless those people would relinquish the right of representation in the

In my many years I have come to a conclusion that one useless man is a shame, two is a law firm, and three or more is a congress.

—JOHN ADAMS

❖❖

Here I am in the state of New Mexico. George Bush is still in the state of denial. New Mexico has five electoral votes. The state of denial has none. I like my chances.

—JOHN KERRY

~❖~

A florist went to a barber for a haircut. After the cut, he asked about his bill, and the barber replied, 'I cannot accept money from you; I'm doing community service this week.' The florist was pleased and left the shop. When the barber went to open his shop the next morning, there was a 'thank you' card and a dozen roses waiting for him at his door.

Later, a cop came in for a haircut, and when he tried to pay his bill, the barber again replied, 'I cannot accept money from you; I'm doing community service this week.' The cop was happy and left the shop.

The next morning when the barber went to open up, there was a 'thank you' card and a dozen donuts waiting for him at his door.

Then a Congressman came in for a haircut, and when he went to pay his bill, the barber again replied, 'I cannot accept money from you. I'm doing community service this week.' The Congressman was very happy and left the shop.

The next morning, when the barber went to open up, there were a dozen Congressmen waiting at the front door.

~✦~

More than 150 heads of state attended the United Nations Summit, giving New Yorkers a chance to get in touch with prejudices they didn't even know they had.

—JON STEWART

✦✦✦

I don't mind what Congress does, as long as they don't do it in the streets and frighten the horses.

—VICTOR HUGO

✦✦

Hell, I never vote for anybody, I always vote against.

—W. C. FIELDS

✦✦✦

ether legislative bodies at places unusual, uncomfortable, and distant from the de-

Ancient Rome declined because it had a Senate; now what's going to happen to us with both a Senate and a House?
—WILL ROGERS

~+~

An admirer of British politician James Hardie made this comment to Winston Churchill: "He is not a great politician, but he will be in heaven before you and me, Winston."

Churchill replied, "If heaven is going to be filled by people like Hardie, the Almighty can have them all to himself."

~+~

We'd all like to vote for the best man, but he's never a candidate.
—KIN HUBBARD

++

I think it's about time we voted for senators with breasts. After all, we've been voting for boobs long enough.
—CLARIE SARGENT

+++

Every two years the American politics industry fills the airwaves with the most virulent, scurrilous, wall-to-wall character assassination of nearly every political practitioner in the country—and then declares itself puzzled that America has lost trust in its politicians.

—CHARLES KRAUTHAMMER

~+~

Mother Jones magazine recently reported that fiscally conservative tea bagger Michele Bachman spent $5000 on hair and makeup when she first launched her Prez run, including a number of $250 haircuts. To which John Edwards muttered, "Amateur."

~+~

I've always said that in politics, your enemies can't hurt you, but your friends will kill you.

—ANN RICHARDS

++

The drinking age should be eighteen. When you're eighteen, you're old enough to vote. You should be old enough to drink. Look who we have to vote for! You need a drink.

—MARK PRICE

+++

ith his measures. ✦ He has dissolved representative houses repeatedly, for opposing

A Higher Power

↔ Although He's regularly asked to do so, God does not take sides in American politics.

↔ If God had meant for us to vote, he would have given us candidates.[4]

↔ If God had been a Liberal, we wouldn't have the 10 Commandments, we'd have the 10 Suggestions.[5]

↔ Asked if he prayed for the senators when he served as the Senate chaplain, Edward Everett Hale replied, " No. I look at the senators and pray for the country."

↔ Why did God create Democrats? To make used car salesmen look good.

↔ Why did God create Republicans? To make used car salesmen look good.

[4] Ice-T
[5] Malcom Bradbury

There were four million people in the Colonies and we had Jefferson, Paine and Franklin. Now we have two hundred and forty million and we have Bush and Quayle. What can you draw from this? Darwin was wrong.

—MORT SAHL

♦♦

Voting in this election is like trying to decide which street mime to stop and watch.

—A.WHITNEY BROWN

♦♦♦

I'd much rather have the fellow inside my tent pissing out, than outside my tent pissing in.

—LYNDON B. JOHNSON

♦♦

I love Barack Obama because when I go to Europe I don't have to pretend to be Canadian any more.

—TOM RHODES

♦♦♦

The President of today is just the postage stamp of tommorrow.

—GRACIE ALLEN

♦♦

ong time, after such dissolutions, to cause others to be elected; whereby the legislative powers, incapable of annihilation, have returned to the people at large for their exercise

the state remaining in the meantime exposed to all the dangers of invasion from with-

REPUBLICANS

It ain't easy bein' a Republican . . . Being a Republican means it's all right to be a bully. After all, God is on your side. Republicans are always right about everything: pro-religion, anti-bureaucracy; pro-military and pro-business. It's their way or the highway (a highway built with American ingenuity, they would add). At the heart of it all? Money. The gathering and keeping of, hereto with . . . It's enough to make you want to . . . well, snark.

What is conservatism? Is it not the adherence to the old and tried against the new and untried?[6]

✦

An honest politician is one who, when he is bought, will stay bought.[7]

✦

Latinos for Republicans. It's like roaches for Raid.[8]

✦

Oh no! The dead have risen and they're voting Republican![9]

✦

GOP: Greed, Oppression, Propaganda.

[6] Abraham Lincoln
[7] Simon Cameron
[8] John Leguizamo
[9] Lisa Simpson

He's not a Republican, he's a Republican't.

✦

Power corrupts, and absolute power is kinda neat.

✦

Under Republicans, man exploits man. Under Democrats, it's exactly the opposite.

✦

Republicans are so empty headed, they wouldn't make a good landfill.[10]

✦

Vote Republican. It's much easier than thinking.

✦

A conservative is one who admires radicals centuries after they're dead.[11]

✦

I'm not a Republican because I don't make enough money to be that big an asshole.[12]

✦

The Republicans' health care plan consists of "'Just say no' to sickness."[13]

✦

Bomb Texas. They have oil!

---

[10] Jim Hightower
[11] Leo Rosten

[12] Paula Poundstone
[13] Kevin Pollack

states; for that purpose obstructing the laws for naturalization of foreigners; refusing

to pass others to encourage their migration hither, and raising the conditions of new

You Call Those Policies?

Politics: "Poli" a Latin word meaning "many"; and "tics"
meaning "bloodsucking creatures.
—ROBIN WILLIAMS

L OOK UP THE WORD "policy." Go ahead.
Aw, forget it, you know I'm gonna tell you anyway.
Policy is defined as a principle or rule to guide decisions with
the ultimate outcome being a rational resolution .... not law,
but a guide . . . a suggestion, if you will . . . usually intended to
help things along . . . everywhere except in politics.

Keep in mind Robin William's astute parsing of the
word politics. Notice both words start with poli. Combined
with "cy," which is Spanish for "yes,"[14] I think it's pretty clear

---

[14]   Go with me on this one.

why so much of government policy is just a reason for politicians to get what they want. Policy is the yes-man of the government system.

But sometimes, my little grasshoppers, another politician—or more likely, his lobbyist— will try to stand in the way. That's when the snarks start to fly.

I don't know what people have got against the government—
they've done nothing.
—BOB HOPE

+++

I'm not a fan of the government doing anything. But I've got
to ask: Why isn't the government doing anything? Maybe
this Ag jobs bill will help. I don't know. Like most members
of Congress, I haven't read it.
—STEPHEN COLBERT

++

I always say gridlock's a good thing . . . it's what the founding
fathers had in mind when they created the Senate.
—BOB DOLE

+++

The government solution to a problem is usually as bad as
the problem.
—MILTON FRIEDMAN

++

Government doesn't solve problems, it subsidizes them.
—RONALD REAGAN

~•~

The National Debt is now over $15 trillion. That's the bad news. The good news is we have enough points for everyone in the country to get a set of luggage.

~•~

The government is unresponsive to the needs of the little man. Under 5'7", it is impossible to get your congressman on the phone.
—WOODY ALLEN

•••

To you taxpayers out there, let me say this: Make sure you file your tax return on time! And remember that, even though income taxes can be a "pain in the neck," the folks at the IRS are regular people just like you, except that they can destroy your life.
—DAVE BARRY

••

If you have ten thousand regulations you destroy all respect for the law.
—WINSTON CHURCHILL

•••

n his will alone, for the tenure of their offices, and the amount and payment of their

~♦~

The neighborhood postman was retiring after 25 years. On his last day of delivering mail, all of the people on his route left him something in the mailbox in honor of his retirement. Some left money, some left small gifts, and some met him at the door and invited him in for a meal. This went on all through the neighborhood. As he proceeded through his route, the gifts got better and better. One house even gave him a gold watch. He was so satisfied, but the last house made all the others pale in comparison. As he was putting the mail in the mailbox, the door opened, and the woman of the house stood there in beautiful lingerie. She invited him inside. He knew that this woman's husband was a truck driver and was away, so he went inside. She proceeded to give him the day and night of his life. The next morning he woke up to find she was bringing him breakfast in bed. He found a dollar bill under his plate as he ate and asked her about it. She explained, "When I called my husband to tell ask him what we should give you for your retirement, he said, 'screw him, give him a dollar.' Breakfast was my idea."

~♦~

The way I understand it, the Russians are sort of a combination of evil and incompetence . . . sort of like the Post Office with tanks.
—EMO PHILIPS

✦✦

Remember one thing about democracy. We can have anything we want and at the same time, we always end up with exactly what we deserve.
—EDWARD ALBEE

✦✦✦

Our goal is to shrink government to the size where we can drown it in a bathtub.
—GROVER NORQUIST

✦✦

Taxation with representation ain't so hot either.
—GERALD BARZAN

✦✦✦

The question is: What can we, as citizens, do to reform our tax system? As you know, under our three-branch system of government, the tax laws are created by: Satan. But he works through the Congress, so that's where we must focus our efforts.
—DAVE BARRY

✦✦✦

We operate under a jury system in this country, and as much as we complain about it, we have to admit that we know of no better system, except possibly flipping a coin.
—DAVE BARRY

✦✦

We have the Bill of Rights. What we need is a Bill of Responsibilities.
—BILL MAHER

✦✦✦

A government that robs Peter to pay Paul can always depend on the support of Paul.
—GEORGE BERNARD SHAW

✦✦

Vote: the instrument and symbol of a freeman's power to make a fool of himself and a wreck of his country.
—AMBROSE BIERCE

~✦~

Bart Simpson: "Didn't you wonder why you were getting checks for doing absolutely nothing?"

Grampa Simpson: "I figured because the democrats were in power again."

~✦~

If anything can go wrong, it will do so in triplicate.
—MURPHY'S LAW AS APPLIED TO GOVERNMENT

+++

Senate office hours are from twelve to one with an hour off
for lunch.
—GEORGE S. KAUFMAN

++

There's nothing in the middle of the road but yellow stripes
and dead armadillos.
—JIM HIGHTOWER

+++

I have wondered at times what the Ten Commandments
would have looked like if Moses had run them through the
US Congress.
—RONALD REAGAN

~+~

*The House voted to reaffirm "In God We
Trust" as the nation's motto, after dismissing
the other contenders, "Yo, we all up in here"
and "Where you at, bee-atches?"*

~+~

We may not imagine how our lives could be more frustrating
and complex—but Congress can.
—CULLEN HIGHTOWER

+++

Congress: Bingo with billions.

—RED SKELTON

++

They say that women talk too much. If you have worked in Congress, you know that the filibuster was invented by men.

—CLARE BOOTHE LUCE

+++

You can lead a man to Congress, but you can't make him think.

—MILTON BERLE

++

Did you ever think that making a speech on economics is a lot like pissing down your leg? It seems hot to you, but it never does to anyone else.

—LYNDON B. JOHNSON

+++

The three-martini lunch is the epitome of American efficiency. Where else can you get an earful, a bellyful and a snootful at the same time?

—GERALD FORD

++

Of course, the truth is that the congresspersons are too busy raising campaign money to read the laws they pass. The laws are written by staff tax nerds who can put pretty much any wording they want in there. I bet that if you actually read the entire vastness of the U.S. tax code, you'd find at least one sex scene. ("Yes, yes, YES!" moaned Vanessa as Lance, his taut body moist with moisture, again and again depreciated her adjusted gross rate of annualized fiscal debenture . . .)

—DAVE BARRY

✦✦✦

When buying and selling are controlled by legislation, the first things to be bought and sold are legislators.

—P. J. O'ROURKE

✦✦

Bureaucracy gives birth to itself and then expects maternity benefits.

—DALE DAUTEN

✦✦✦

The White House looked into a plan that would allow illegal immigrants to stay in the United States. The plan called for a million Mexicans to marry a million of our ugliest citizens.

—DENNIS MILLER

✦✦

How the United States Government Does Business Today

A small town in the United States and the place looks almost totally deserted. It is tough times, everybody is in debt, and everybody lives on credit. Suddenly, a rich tourist comes to town. He enters the town's only hotel, lays $100 on the reception counter as a deposit, and goes to inspect the rooms upstairs in order to pick one. What happens?

1. The hotel proprietor takes the money and runs to pay his debt to the butcher.
2. The butcher takes the money and runs to pay his debt to the pig farmer.
3. The pig farmer pays the supplier of his feed and fuel.
4. The supplier of feed and fuel pay off his escort fees.
5. The escort service pays the hotel for the rooms she rented for clients.
6. The hotel proprietor puts the money back on the counter so that the rich tourist will not suspect anything.

At that moment, the tourist comes down after inspecting the rooms, and takes back his money, saying that he did not like any of the rooms. He leaves town.

No one earned anything . . . However, the whole town is now without debt, and looks to the future with a lot of optimism.

Blessed are the young, for they shall inherit the national debt.
—HERBERT HOOVER

✦✦✦

The only difference between a taxman and a taxidermist is that the taxidermist leaves the skin.
—MARK TWAIN

✦✦

I contend that for a nation to try to tax itself into prosperity is like a man standing in a bucket and trying to lift himself up by the handle.
—WINSTON CHURCHILL

✦✦✦

Foreign aid might be defined as a transfer of money from poor people in rich countries to rich people in poor countries.
—DOUGLAS CASEY

✦✦

rom punishment for any murders which they should commit on the inhabitants of these

Take away the right to say "fuck" and you take away the
right to say "fuck the government".
—LENNY BRUCE

~•~

*Herbert Hoover once complained to former
president Calvin Coolidge that his attempts to
promote economic recovery during the Great
Depression seemed to be having minimal
impact; moreover, his critics were becoming
increasingly vocal and belligerent. "You can't
expect to see calves running in the field the day
after you put the bull to the cows," Coolidge
remarked. "No," Hoover replied. "But I would
at least expect to see contented cows."*

~•~

Government is the great fiction, through which everybody
endeavors to live at the expense of everybody else.
—FREDERIC BASTIAT

•••

It was my fortune, or misfortune, to be called to the office of
Chief Executive without any previous political training.
—ULYSSES S. GRANT

••

Government's view of the economy could be summed up in a few short phrases: If it moves, tax it. If it keeps moving, regulate it. And if it stops moving, subsidize it.
—RONALD REAGAN

♦♦♦

In general, the art of government consists of taking as much money as possible from one party of the citizens to give to the other.
—VOLTAIRE

♦♦

All governments suffer a recurring problem: Power attracts pathological personalities.
—FRANK HERBERT

~♦~

The latter portion of Jimmy Carter's presidency was plagued by recession. The American economy did not pick up again until Ronald Reagan had assumed the helm (in the early 1980s).

"Depression is when you are out of work," Reagan declared after taking office. "Recession is when your neighbor is out of work . . . "

And a recovery? "A recovery is when Jimmy Carter is out of work!"

~♦~

Ann Richards on How to Be a Good Republican:

1. You have to believe that the nation's current eight-year prosperity was due to the work of Ronald Reagan and George Bush, but yesterday's gasoline prices are all Clinton's fault.
2. You have to believe that those privileged from birth achieve success all on their own.
3. You have to be against all government programs, but expect Social Security checks on time.

A President needs political understanding to run the government, but he may be elected without it.
—HARRY S. TRUMAN

✦✦✦

I don't know whether it's the finest public housing in America or the crown jewel of the federal prison system.
—BILL CLINTON [ON LIVING IN THE WHITE HOUSE]

✦✦

When we got into office, the thing that surprised me the most was that things were as bad as we'd been saying they were.
—JOHN F. KENNEDY

✦✦✦

I am a high-priced Washington lobbyist peddling influence
. . . Who wants candy?
—FAMILY GUY

++

Can any of you seriously say the Bill of Rights could
get through Congress today? It wouldn't even get out of
committee.
—F. LEE BAILEY

+++

Socialist: a person who is so disgusted by the way power is
controlled by a few huge corporations that he proposes to
place it in the hands of one giant corporation.

++

People want to say there isn't racial profiling at the airport,
but let's be honest. If you first name is Mohammed, and your
last name isn't Ali, leave a little extra time.
—JAY LENO

+++

A Homeland Security official was arrested for soliciting
sex from a teenager, who was actually a cop on the Internet.
Some of their chats went on for hours, because you know
Homeland Security, they take forever to come.
—BILL MAHER

++

shing the free system of English laws in a neighboring province, establishing therein an

The Department of Homeland Security recommends a three-day supply of water consisting of one bottle per day for each person in your home. Plus one extra bottle to give you all something to kill each other over on day four.

—JON STEWART

+++

Tom Ridge set up a five-stage, color-coded system to warn Americans against threats. The colors are green, blue, yellow, orange and red. This is what the Republicans meant when they said they are trying to get more color in the party ... This thing is so confusing. Yesterday the alert went from blue to pink; now half the country thinks we're pregnant.

—JAY LENO

++

If you want somebody to repair your roads, educate your kids, or purify your water supply, you may want to turn to private enterprise, but if you want massive f***loads of your enemies wiped out in record time, Uncle Sam is the man for you.

—DENNIS MILLER

+++

He could shake your hand and stab you in the back at the same time.

—HUNTER S. THOMPSON ON RICHARD NIXON

++

arbitrary government, and enlarging its boundaries so as to render it at once an example

Policy is the name we give to our future mistakes.
—HENRY WALLICH

~♦~

Hey Congress: What to do, what to do . . . the economy's is in the toilet, we're still in at least two wars (that we know of), unemployment's at the highest it's been in years, our reputation has been damaged throughout the world and we may no longer be considered a superpower . . . but hey, I know! Let's sign a pledge against gay marriage . . .

~♦~

All the problems we face in the United States today can be traced to an unenlightened immigration policy on the part of the American Indian.
—PAT PAULSEN

♦♦♦

The wages of sin are death, but by the time taxes are taken out, it's just sort of a tired feeling.
—PAULA POUNDSTONE

♦♦

You don't pay taxes—they take taxes.
—CHRIS ROCK

♦♦♦

~•~

They say if you give a man a fish, he'll eat for a day, but if you teach a man to fish . . . . then he's gotta get a fishing license, but he doesn't have any money. So he's got to get a job and get into the Social Security system and pay taxes, and now you're gonna audit the poor cocksucker, 'cause he's not really good with math. So the IRS van will pull up to his house, and they'll take all his shit. They'll take his black velvet Elvis and his Batman toothbrush, and his penis pump, and that all goes up for auction with the burden of proof on him because he forgot to carry the one, 'cause he was just worried about eating a fucking fish, and he couldn't even cook the fish 'cause he needed a permit for an open flame. Then the Health Department is going to start asking him a lot of questions about where he's going to dump the scales and the guts. 'This is not a sanitary environment,' and if he gets sick of it all at the end of the day . . . it's not even legal to kill himself in this country.

You were born free, you got fucked out of half of it, and you wave a flag celebrating it. Hey, the only true freedom you find, is when you realize and come to terms with the fact that you are completely and unapologetically fucked, and then you are free to float around the system.

—Doug Stanhope

~◆~

Freedom of Press is limited to those who own one.
—H. L. MENCKEN

◆◆

Censorship is telling a man he can't have a steak just because a baby can't chew it.
—MARK TWAIN

◆◆◆

Don't think of it as 'gun control,' think of it as 'victim disarmament.' If we make enough laws, we can all be criminals.

◆◆

Illegal aliens have always been a problem in the United States. Ask any Indian.
—ROBERT ORBEN

◆◆◆

rms of our governments: ◆ For suspending our own legislatures, and declaring them-

~✦~

In Ronald Reagan's first televised budget speech as president, he used a handful of change to illustrate the current value of the dollar.

"It takes an actor to do that," remarked a rival Democrat with grudging admiration. "Carter would have emphasized all the wrong words. Ford would have fumbled and dropped the cash. And Nixon would have pocketed it."

~✦~

Drugs. If they did not exist our governors would have invented them in order to prohibit them and so make much of the population vulnerable to arrest, imprisonment, seizure of property, and so on.

—GORE VIDAL

✦✦

A drug is neither moral nor immoral—it's a chemical compound. The compound itself is not a menace to society until a human being treats it as if consumption bestowed a temporary license to act like an asshole.

—FRANK ZAPPA

✦✦✦

Republicans are against abortion until their daughters need one, Democrats are for abortion until their daughter wants one.

—GRACE MCGARVIE

++

Abortion is advocated only by persons who have themselves been born.

—RONALD REAGAN

+++

If men could get pregnant, abortion would be a sacrament.

—FLORENCE KENNEDY

++

The income tax created more criminals than any other single act of government.

—BARRY M. GOLDWATER

++

This battle for 'common-sense' gun control laws pits emotion and passion against logic and reason. All too often in such a contest, logic loses. So, expect more meaningless, if not harmful, 'gun control' legislation. Good news—if you're a crook.

—LARRY ELDER

+++

Did you know America ranks the lowest in education but the highest in drug use? It's nice to be number one, but we can fix that. All we need to do is start the war on education. If it's anywhere near as successful as our war on drugs, in no time we'll all be hooked on phonics.

—LEIGHANN LORD

♦♦

Why is pot against the law? It wouldn't be because anyone can grow it, and therefore you can't make a profit off it, would it?

—BILL HICKS

♦♦♦

There is a war on drugs, but I surrendered.

—MARILYN MANSON

♦♦

If a tree falls in the woods, and there's no one there to hear it, how will the Environmentalists react?

—ANONYMOUS

♦♦♦

Whatever it is that the government does, sensible Americans would prefer that the government does it to somebody else. This is the idea behind foreign policy.

—P. J. O'ROURKE

♦♦

has plundered our seas, ravaged our coasts, burned our towns, and destroyed the live

Blame the Government for . . .

- ↦ The financial crisis
- ↦ Rude department store/ DMV/ Post Office/ Starbucks employees
- ↦ People who don't clean up after their dog
- ↦ Tailgaters
- ↦ Spam
- ↦ Oil spills
- ↦ Our celebrity-obsessed culture[15]
- ↦ Never-ending television ads
- ↦ Pay toilets
- ↦ The military industrial complex
- ↦ Fat people stuffing their faces at McDonalds
- ↦ Junk mail
- ↦ The bank bailout

---

[15] Actually, make that everything bad about the culture.

our people. ◆ He is at this time transporting large armies of foreign mercenaries

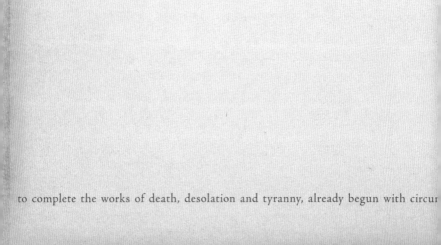
to complete the works of death, desolation and tyranny, already begun with circum

ances of cruelty and perfidy scarcely paralleled in the most barbarous ages, and totally

DEMOCRATS

It ain't easy bein' a Democrat . . . reaching out blindly, knowing what you want but not how to get it . . . that's a Democrat. Being a Democrat means you're only ever so slightly to the right of being a Liberal. You think the Bill of Rights might be "a little outdated." You smoked pot once, in college, and may have inhaled but "don't really remember, it was all a blur." You love NPR and PBS. You "really miss" the 60's, even if you were born 10 years after they were over. At the heart of it, mostly what Democrats are, are easy targets. Observe.

I am not a member of any organized political party. I am a Democrat.[16]

If you get 15 democrats in a room, you'll get 20 opinions.[17]

Government stimulates the Democratic party.[18]

Bipartisanship. I'll hug your elephant if you'll kiss my ass.

---

[16] Will Rogers   [17] Patrick Leahy   [18] Rush Limbaugh

I never said all Democrats were saloonkeepers. What I said was that all saloonkeepers are Democrats.[19]

✦

Democrats: Cleaning Up Republican Messes Since 1933

✦

I'd rather go hunting with Cheney, than go driving with Ted Kennedy

Vote Democrat— it's easier than working!

✦

The media are only as liberal as the conservative businesses that own them.

✦

You have to have been a Republican to know how good it is to be a Democrat.[20]

✦

I'm too poor to vote Republican.

[19] Horace Greeley   [20] Jackie Kennedy

aptive on the high seas to bear arms against their country, to become the executioners

of their friends and brethren, or to fall themselves by their hands. ⁕ He has excited do

Below the Belt

It has been the political career of this man to begin
with hypocrisy, proceed with arrogance, and finish with
contempt.
—THOMAS PAINE [ON JOHN ADAMS]

"C MON . . . BRING THE nasty."
Reading those four words, one is hard pressed to
know if the speaker is talking about Baseball, reciting lyrics
from some new rap ditty . . . or throwing down the gauntlet in
a politic debate. Take my word for it . . . 8 out of 10 times, it's
most definitely about Politics.

More often than not, the easiest way that one candidate
chooses to attack another (short of challenging an opponent
to a duel[21]) is by focusing the country's attention on the opponent's shortcomings—his/her appearance, speech, knowledge (or lack thereof), grammar, height, weight, hair . . .
anything but where he or she stands on the issues. Sometime

---

[21] As Aaron Burr said, " Been there, done that."

nestic insurrections amongst us, and has endeavored to bring on the inhabitants of our

back around the early days of the constitution, it all became fair game . . . open season . . . the gloves came off . . . everything goes . . . and it continues to this day.

The problem seems to be with the level of discourse. Most of the attacks nowadays tend toward the base and common. Back in the day[22], people were much more clever with their bile.

Bush gave an interview and said people will vote for him because "They've seen me weep, they've seen me laugh, and they've seen me hug." These are the same qualifications for a Tickle Me Elmo.

—BILL MAHER

++

Bill Clinton is most comfortable when thinking about little things—school uniforms, the minimum wage, and above all, himself.

—GEORGE WILL

+++

Ronald Reagan is the first president to be accompanied by a Silly Statement Repair team.

—MARK RUSSELL

++

---

22 He didn't just use that old saw, did he?

frontiers, the merciless Indian savages, whose known rule of warfare, is undistinguishe

A POLITICIAN IS . . .

. . . a fellow who will lay down your life for his country.
—TEXAS GUINAN

✦✦✦

. . . like quicksilver: if you try to put your finger on him, you find nothing under it. —AUSTIN O'MALLEY

✦✦

. . . a person who approaches every subject with an open mouth. —ADLAI STEVENSON

✦✦✦

. . . a man who can be verbose in fewer words than anybody else. —PETER DE VRIES

✦✦

. . . .a biped; but he is probably an aberrant form of hyena.
—ABRAHAM MILLER

Bush is unusually incurious, abnormally unintelligent, amazingly inarticulate, fantastically uncultured, extraordinarily uneducated, and apparently quite proud of all these things.
—CHRISTOPHER HITCHENS

✦✦

A pin-stripin' polo-playin' umbrella-totin' Ivy-leaguer, born with a silver spoon so far in his mouth that you couldn't get it out with a crowbar.
—BILL BAXLEY [ON GEORGE BUSH]

✦✦✦

estruction of all ages, sexes and conditions. ✦ In every stage of these oppressions we

He doesn't die his hair, he bleaches his face.
—JOHNNY CARSON [ABOUT REAGAN]

♦♦

He is your typical, smiling, brilliant, back stabbing,
bullshitting southern nut-cutter.
—LANE KIRKLAND [ON JIMMY CARTER]

♦♦♦

He looks like the guy in a science fiction movie who is the
first to see the Creature.
—DAVID FRYE [ON GERALD FORD]

♦♦

The enviably attractive nephew who sings an Irish ballad for
the company and then winsomely disappears before the table
clearing and dishwashing begins.
—LYNDON B. JOHNSON [ON JOHN F. KENNEDY]

♦♦♦

General Eisenhower has dedicated himself so many times he
must feel like the cornerstone of a public building.
—ADLAI STEVENSON

♦♦

Hoover isn't a stuffed shirt. But at times he can give the most
convincing impersonation of a stuffed shirt you ever saw.
—ANON

♦♦♦

Calvin Coolidge didn't say much, and when he did, he didn't say much.

—WILL ROGERS

◆◆

On Warren Harding

He writes the worst English that I have ever encountered. It reminds me of a string of wet sponges; it reminds me of tattered washing on the line; it reminds me of stale bean soup, of dogs barking idiotically through endless nights. It drags itself out of the dark abysm of pish and crawls insanely up the topmost pinnacle of posh. It is rumble and bumble. It is flap and doodle. It is balder and dash.

—H. L. MENCKEN

◆◆◆

His speeches left the impression of an army of pompous phrases moving over the landscape in search of an idea.

—WILLIAM MCADOO

◆◆

A tinhorn politician with the manner of a rural corn doctor and the mien of a ham actor.

—H. L. MENCKEN

◆◆◆

nswered only by repeated injury. A prince, whose character is thus marked by every act

Two thirds mush and one-third Eleanor.
—ALICE ROOSEVELT LONGWORTH [ON THEODORE
ROOSEVELT]

••

A non-entity with side whiskers.
—WOODROW WILSON [ON CHESTER ARTHUR]

•••

He looked at me as if I was a side dish he hadn't ordered.
—RING LARDNER [ON WILLIAM TAFT]

••

He has no more backbone than a chocolate éclair.
—LOUISE LAMPREY [ON WILLIAM MCKINLEY]

•••

He sailed through American history like a steel ship loaded
with monoliths of granite.
—H. L. MENCKEN [ON GROVER CLEVELAND]

••

He rushes into a fight with the horns of a bull and the skin
of a rabbit.
—JEREMIAH BLACK [ON JAMES GARFIELD]

••

A bloated mass of political putridity.
—THADDEUS STEVENS [ON JAMES BUCHANAN]

•••

MATCH THE PRESIDENT TO THE INSULT[23]

A. George Bush

B. Jimmy Carter

C. Richard Nixon

D. Theodore
   Roosevelt

E. Calvin Coolidge

F. George Washington

G. Bill Clinton

H. Dwight
   Eisenhower

~+~

1. A sordid, ambitious, vain, arrogant, and vindictive knave. [General Charles Lee]

2. Calling him shallow is like calling a dwarf short. [Molly Ivins]

3. I worship the quicksand he walks on. [Art Buchwald]

4. He looks as though he'd been weaned on a pickle. [Alice R. Longworth]

5. An old maid with testosterone poisoning. [Patricia O'Tolle]

6. When he gave a fireside chat, the fire went out. [Anon]

7. Once he makes up his mind, he's full of indecision. [Oscar Levant]

8. It's the first time he's ever rejected pussy. [G. Gordon Liddy, when _____ gave away his cat.]

---

[23] 1.F., 2.A., 3.C., 4.E., 5.D., 6.B., 7.H., 8.G.

Van Buren struts and swaggers like a crow in the gutter. He is laced up in corsets . . . it would be difficult to say whether he was a man or a woman.

—DAVY CROCKETT

✦✦

A commonplace man of no great brilliance.

—ALICE DURANT [ON JAMES MONROE]

✦✦✦

He is a bewildered, confounded, and miserably perplexed man.

—ABRAHAM LINCOLN [ON JAMES POLK]

✦✦

A barbarian who could not write a sentence of grammar and hardly could spell his own name.

—JOHN QUINCY ADAMS [ON ANDREW JACKSON]

✦✦✦

His disposition is as perverse and mulish as that of his father.

—JAMES BUCHANAN [ON JOHN QUINCY ADAMS]

✦✦✦

First in ability on the list of second-rate men.

—NY TIMES [ON CHESTER ARTHUR]

✦✦

His principles are all subordinate to his ambitions.

—JOHN QUINCY ADAMS [ON MARTIN VAN BUREN]

✦✦

of attempts by their legislature to extend an unwarrantable jurisdiction over us. V

My father always wanted to be the center of attention.
When he went to a wedding, he wanted to be the
bridegroom. When he went to a funeral, he wanted to be the
corpse.
—ALICE ROOSEVELT LONGWORTH

✦✦✦

You have all the characteristics of a popular politician: a
horrible voice, bad breeding, and a vulgar manner.
—ARISTOPHANES

✦✦

Once there were two brothers. One ran away to sea; the
other was elected vice president of the United States. And
nothing was heard of either of them ever again.
—THOMAS MARSHALL, VP TO WOODROW WILSON

✦✦✦

He is going around the country stirring up apathy.
—WILLIAM WHITELAW [ON HAROLD WILSON]

✦✦

He is but a withered little apple-john.
—WASHINGTON IRVING [ON JAMES MADISON]

✦✦✦

Thomas Jefferson's slaves loved him so much they called him
by a special name: Dad.
—MARK RUSSELL

✦✦✦

ve reminded them of the circumstances of our emigration and settlement here. We

His Rotundity.
—ANON [ON JOHN ADAMS]

++

The vice-presidency ain't worth a pitcher of warm spit.
—VP JOHN NANCE GARNER

++

Such a little man could not have made so big a depression.
—NORMAN THOMAS [ON HERBERT HOOVER]

++

On Fox News, they address her as Governor Palin . . . that's like calling me a 'Dairy Queen employee.' I was once, but I quit.
—TINA FEY

+++

If Hillary gave up one of her balls and gave it to Obama, he'd have two.
—JAMES CARVILLE

++

The definition of redundancy is an airbag in a politician's car.
—LARRY HAGMAN

+++

Everything is changing. People are taking their comedians seriously and the politicians as a joke.
—WILL ROGERS

+++

have appealed to their native justice and magnanimity, and we have conjured them

I don't make jokes. I just watch the government and report the facts.

—WILL ROGERS

✦✦

People say I'm ruthless. I am not ruthless . . . and if I find the SOB that's calling me ruthless, I will destroy him.

—BOBBY KENNEDY

✦✦✦

When Bob Dole does smile, he looks as if he's just evicted a widow.

—MIKE ROYKO

~✦~

Edward Kennedy once went to probate court to have his name changed. "One brother is President and the other is Attorney General. I want a name not so politically known".

The judge asked him what name he wanted instead of Teddy Kennedy. He replied, "Oh, I'd like to keep Teddy and change the last name to Roosevelt".

~✦~

Mike Dukakis radiates all the studly presidential command of Rocket J. Squirrel.
—OWEN GLEIBERMAN

❖❖❖

John Glenn couldn't electrify a fish tank if he threw a toaster in it.
—DAVE BARRY

❖❖

Al Gore is like the fat boy in the schoolyard. Tormenting him is so much fun, nobody can resist . . . a natural-born victim.
—RUSSELL BAKER

❖❖❖

I can still remember the first time I heard Hubert Humphrey speak. He was in the second hour of a five-minute talk.
—GERALD FORD

❖❖

Walter Mondale has all the charisma of a speed bump.
—WILL DURST

❖❖❖

I told Mr. Nader today that a vote for Ralph Nader is really a vote for George Bush.
—BARBARA LEE

❖❖

MATCH THE PRESIDENT TO HIS DESCRIPTION[24]

A. Gerald Ford   D. Herbert Hoover
B. William Taft   E. Woodrow Wilson
C. William Henry
   Harrison

~+~

1. A flub-dub with a streak of the second-rate and the common. [Theodore Roosevelt]
2. Our President Imbecile Chief. [Andrew Jackson]
3. The air currents of the world never ventilated his mind. [Walter Page]
4. So dumb, he can't fart and chew gum at the same time. [Lyndon B. Johnson]
5. The man offered me unsolicited advice for six years, all of it bad. [Calvin Coolidge]

---

[24] 1.B., 2.C., 3.E., 4.A., 5.D.

stice and of consanguinity. We must, therefore, acquiesce in the necessity, which de-

Thomas Dewey is the only man able to walk under a bed without hitting his head.
—WALTER WINCHELL

+++

After a quick meet-and-greet with King Abdullah, Obama was off to Israel, where he made a quick stop at the manger in Bethlehem where he was born.
—JON STEWART, ON BARACK OBAMA'S MIDDLE EAST TRIP

++

Winston Churchill would kill his own mother just so he could use her skin to make a drum to beat his own praises.
—MARGOT ASQUITH

+++

In politics if you want anything said, ask a man. If you want anything done, ask a woman.
—MARGARET THATCHER

++

She ate journalists for breakfast and, feeling peckish, bit off some reporters' heads at a press conference.
—TREVOR FISHLOCK [ON MARGARET THATCHER]

+++

It takes a certain kind of man to be in politics—a small one.
—CROFT M. PENTZ

++

Winston Churchill[25]

*On General Montgomery: "In defeat unbeatable, in victory unbearable."

*On former Prime Minister Stanley Baldwin: "He occasionally stumbled over the truth, but hastily picked himself up and hurried on as if nothing had happened."

*A woman who had just heard a recent speech made by Winston Churchill asked him,

" Doesn't it thrill you that every time you make a speech the hall is packed to overflowing?" Churchill replied, " Whenever I feel that way I always remember that if I was being hanged instead, the crowd would be twice as big."

*Told that familiarity breeds contempt, Churchill responded, "I would remind you that without a degree of familiarity we could not breed anything."

*"He can best be described as one of those orators who, before they get up, do not know what they are going to say; when they are speaking, do not know what they are saying; and, when they have sat down, do not know what they have said."

*"Mr. Churchill, can you tell me how I could have put more fire into my speech?"

"What you should have done is put your speech into the fire."

---

[25] The Brits just have a way with words.

~•~

Though touted as a candidate for his party's nomination in the 2004 presidential election, many Democrats fretted about John Edwards' distinct lack of foreign policy experience. "Why," whispered Mr. Gore's friends, "should the party drop a former congressman, senator and vice-president for an untried newcomer— whose only experience of foreign affairs consists of visits to the International House of Pancakes?"

~•~

The President needs a break. He's like a Black & Decker vacuum. If you don't recharge his batteries, he can't suck.
—STEPHEN COLBERT

••

I see that one of my opponents has lost his head.
—WILLIAM TAFT AFTER A HECKLER THREW A CABBAGE AT HIM DURING A SPEECH.

••

If you call your opponent a politician, it's grounds for libel.
—MARK RUSSELL

•••

in General Congress, assembled, appealing to the Supreme Judge of the world for th

Paul Keating[26]

*I am not the leader of the Opposition. I did not slither out of the Cabinet like a mangy maggot.

*What we have here is an intellectual rust bucket.

*A gutless spiv . . . a painted perfumed gigolo . . . the Liberal Party ought to put him down like a faithful dog because he is of no use to it of no use to the nation.

*What we have as a leader of the national Party is a political carcass with a coat and tie on.

*All tip and no iceberg.

Malcolm Fraser is the cutlery man of Australia. He was born with a silver spoon in his mouth, speaks with a forked tongue and knifes his colleagues in the back.

—BOB HAWKE

~◆~

An elderly lady once approached Gerald Ford after he had given an address.

"I hear you spoke here tonight" she said.

Ford, always modest, said, "Oh, it was nothing."

"Yes" she replied, "that's what I heard."

~◆~

---

[26] He was the Prime Minister of Australia from 1991 to 1996. If you think it's too obscure, complain to my publisher. Please.

~+~

While Governor of New Jersey, Woodrow Wilson, received word that one of the state's senators had died. Within minutes, he got a called from another politician who told Wilson, "I would like to take the senator's place." Wilson replied, "That is perfectly agreeable to me if agreeable to the undertaker."

~+~

I think this is the most extraordinary collection of talent, of human knowledge, that has ever been gathered at the White House—with the possible exception of when Thomas Jefferson dined alone.

—JOHN F. KENNEDY

++

We in the Republican party have never said to the press that Clinton's a philandering, pot-smoking draft-dodger.

—MARY MATALIN

++

Anyone who extends to him the right hand of friendship is in danger of losing a couple of fingers.

—ALVA JOHNSTON [ON FIORELLO LA GUARDIA]

+++

these colonies, solemnly publish and declare, that these united colonies are, and of righ

If Nixon is alone in a room, is anyone there?
—GLORIA STEINEM

••

The battle for the mind of Ronald Reagan was like trench warfare in World War One; never have so many fought so hard for such barren terrain.
—PEGGY NOONAN

~•~

Hubert Humphrey, known to be quite verbose, was told by his wife Muriel, "Hubert, a speech, to be immortal, doesn't have to be eternal."

~•~

As the leader of twelve apostles, even Jesus had more executive experience than Obama.
—ANN COULTER

•••

ught to be free and independent states; that they are absolved from all allegiance to the

British Crown, and that all political connection between them and the state of Grea

Musing Philosophic

Being president is like being a jackass in a hailstorm. There's
nothing to do but stand there and take it.
—LYNDON JOHNSON

THERE'S A CLASSIC QUOTE that's always been credited to Mae West—"Marriage is an institution . . . but I'm not ready for an institution just yet." Well, Politics and Government are also institutions . . . and, believe me, no one is ever ready for them.

Yes, it takes a certain caliber of American to look at every aspect of the political arena, assess the field, decide upon one's morals and principles . . . and resist public service. Those that can't resist, run for office.

It also takes a special kind of political animal to do the same reconnaissance and come away with a decision to "throw my hat in the ring." A heady mix of ego, bluster, swagger, "cojones," and arrogance . . . pour into blender, add a healthy dose of good looks and 500 kilowatt smile and you have that creature known as . . . The Candidate.

ritain, is and ought to be totally dissolved; and that as free and independent states,

Cast your eyes upon him/her . . . but be careful you don't turn to stone.

Disbelief in magic can force a poor soul into believing in government and business.
—TOM ROBBINS

••

Never underestimate the ego of a politician.
—DAN BROWN

••

The men the American people admire most extravagantly are the most daring liars: the men they detest most violently are those that try to tell the truth.
—H. L. MENCKEN

•••

The American political system is like fast food—mushy, insipid, made out of disgusting parts of things . . . and everybody wants some.
—P. J. O'ROURKE

•••

Politics is a blood sport.
—ANEURIN BEVAN

✦✦

In politics, nothing happens by accident. If it happens, you
can bet it was planned that way.
—FRANKLIN DELANO ROOSEVELT

✦✦✦

Power draws the corrupted; absolute power would draw the
absolutely corrupted.
—COLIN BARTH

✦✦

One of the little celebrated powers of Presidents is to listen
to their critics with just enough sympathy to ensure their
silence.
—JOHN GALBRAITH

✦✦✦

When I was a boy I was told that anybody could become
President; I'm beginning to believe it.
—CLARENCE DARROW

✦✦

Man cannot live by bread alone; he must have peanut butter.
—JAMES A. GARFIELD

✦✦✦

POLITICS IS . . .

. . . the art of looking for trouble, finding it whether it exists or not, diagnosing it incorrectly, and applying the wrong remedy.
—GROUCHO MARX

+++

. . . the skilled use of blunt objects.
—LESTER B PEARSON

++

. . . made up largely of irrelevancies.
—DALTON CAMP

+++

. . . perhaps the only profession for which no preparation is thought necessary.
—ROBERT LOUIS STEVENSON

++

. . . the art of preventing people from sticking their noses in things that are properly their business.
—PAUL VALERY

+++

. . . the art of postponing decisions until they are no longer relevant.
—HENRI QUEUILLE

++

. . . supposed to be the second oldest profession. I have come to realize that it bears a very close resemblance to the first.
—RONALD REAGAN

✦✦✦

. . . is like football; if you see daylight, go through the hole.
—JOHN F. KENNEDY

Politics is not a bad profession. If you succeed there are many rewards, if you disgrace yourself . . . you can always write a book.
—RONALD REAGAN

✦✦✦

Politics is not the art of the impossible. It consists in choosing between the disastrous and the unpalatable.
—JOHN KENNETH GAILBRAITH

✦✦

The right to be heard does not automatically include the right to be taken seriously.
—HUBERT HUMPHREY

✦✦

I always figured the American public wanted a solemn ass for President, so I went along with them.
—CALVIN COOLIDGE

✦✦✦

ence, we mutually pledge to each other our lives, our fortunes and our sacred honor.

The vice-presidency is like the last cookie on the plate. Everybody insists he won't take it, but somebody always does.
—BILL VAUGHAN

✦✦

The man with the best job in the country is the Vice President. All he has to do is get up every morning and say, "How's the President?"
—WILL ROGERS

✦✦✦

When a man assumes a public trust, he should consider himself as public property.
—THOMAS JEFFERSON

✦✦

Always be sincere, even if you don't mean it.
—HARRY S. TRUMAN

✦✦✦

A fool and his money are soon elected.
—WILL ROGERS

✦✦

Everybody knows politics is a contact sport.
—BARACK OBAMA

✦✦✦

Forgive your enemies, but never forget their names.
—JOHN F. KENNEDY

✦✦

On Democracy

Democracy means government by discussion, but it is only effective if you can stop people talking.
—CLEMENT ATLEE

+++

Democracy is a process by which the people are free to choose the man who will get all the blame.
—LAURENCE J. PETER

++

The best argument against democracy is a five-minute conversation with the average voter.
—WINSTON CHURCHILL

+++

I believe democracy is our greatest export. At least until China figures out a way to stamp it out of plastic for three cents a unit.
—STEPHEN COLBERT

+++

Democracy means simply the bludgeoning of the people by the people for the people.
—OSCAR WILDE

++

Democracy substitutes election by the incompetent many for appointment by the corrupt few.
—GEORGE BERNARD SHAW

Mothers all want their sons to grow up to be president but they don't want them to become politicians in the process.
—JOHN F. KENNEDY

Being president is like running a cemetery: you've got a lot of people under you and nobody's listening.
—BILL CLINTON

I have no ambition to govern men; it is a painful and thankless office.
—THOMAS JEFFERSON

All the president is . . . is a glorified public relations man who spends his time flattering, kissing, and kicking people to get them to do what they are supposed to do anyway.
—HARRY S. TRUMAN

The pay is good and I can walk to work.
—JOHN F. KENNEDY

Oh, that lovely title, ex-president.
—DWIGHT D. EISENHOWER

Capitalism is the astounding belief that the most wickedest of men will do the most wickedest of things for the greatest good of everyone.
—JOHN MAYNARD KEYNES

Apparently, a democracy is a place where numerous elections are held at great cost without issues and with interchangeable candidates.
—GORE VIDAL

••

The office of president is such a bastardized thing, half royalty and half democracy that nobody knows whether to genuflect or spit.
—JIMMY BRESLIN

•••

Trying to get the presidency to work these days is like trying to sew buttons on a custard pie.
—JAMES BARBER

••

Those that are too smart to engage in politics are punished by being governed by those who are dumber.
—PLATO

•••

I have come to the conclusion that politics is too serious a matter to be left to the politicians.
—CHARLES DEGAULLE

••

A man's got to believe in something. I believe I'll have another drink.
—W. C. FIELDS

•••

the States, having at the time of their adopting the Constitution, expressed a desire,

A politician should have three hats. One for throwing into the ring, one for talking through, and one for pulling rabbits out of if elected.

—CARL SANDBURG

+++

Any American who is prepared to run for president should automatically, by definition, be disqualified from ever doing so.

—GORE VIDAL

++

One of the penalties for refusing to participate in politics is that you end up being governed by your inferiors.

—PLATO

+++

There is one thing about being President—no one can tell you when to sit down.

—DWIGHT D. EISENHOWER

++

Democracy is the art and science of running the circus from the monkey cage.

—H. L. MENCKEN

+++

There's nothing left . . . but to get drunk.
—FRANKLIN PIERCE,
AFTER LOSING THE DEMOCRATIC NOMINATION

++

Political language. . . is designed to make lies sound truthful
and murder respectable, and to give an appearance of
solidity to pure wind.
—GEORGE ORWELL

+++

In the lexicon of the political class, the word "sacrifice"
means that the citizens are supposed to mail even more of
their income to Washington so that the political class will
not have to sacrifice the pleasure of spending it.
—GEORGE WILL

++

Society is like a stew. If you don't stir it up every once in a
while then a layer of scum floats to the top.
—EDWARD ABBEY

+++

Politics makes estranged bedfellows.
—GOODMAN ACE

++

estrictive clauses should be added: And as extending the ground of public confidence in

If a tree falls in a forest and lands on a politician, even if you can't hear the tree or the screams, I'll bet you'd at least hear the applause.

—PAUL TINDALE

✦✦✦

It has been said that democracy is the worst form of government except all the others that have been tried.

—WINSTON CHURCHILL

✦✦

You want a friend in Washington? Get a dog.

—HARRY S. TRUMAN

✦✦✦

Patriotism is a pernicious, psychopathic form of idiocy.

—GEORGE BERNARD SHAW

✦✦

If you can't convince them, confuse them.

—HARRY TRUMAN

✦✦✦

When you reach the end of your rope, tie a knot in it and hang on.

—THOMAS JEFFERSON

✦✦

Now I know what a statesman is; he's a dead politician. We
need more statesmen.
—BOB EDWARDS

+++

The politicians were talking themselves red, white and blue
in the face.
—CLARE BOOTHE LUCE

++

Battle, n. A method of untying with the teeth a political
knot that would not yield to the tongue.
—AMBROSE BIERCE

+++

Frankly, I don't mind not being President. I just mind that
someone else is.
—EDWARD KENNEDY

++

Turn on to politics, or politics will turn on you.
—RALPH NADER

+++

Politicians are wonderful people as long as they stay away from
things they don't understand, such as working for a living.
—P. J. O'ROURKE

+++

the Senate and House of Representatives of the United States of America, in

Who Knows Who Said It?[27]

How come we choose from just two people to run for president and 50 for Miss America?

To succeed in politics, it is often necessary to rise above your principles.

Any sufficiently advanced bureaucracy is indistinguishable from molasses.

You know, sometimes, when they say you're ahead of your time, it's just a polite way of saying you have a real bad sense of timing.

—GEORGE MCGOVERN

++

The whole aim of practical politics is to keep the populace alarmed (and hence clamorous to be led to safety) by menacing it with an endless series of hobgoblins, all of them imaginary.

—H. L. MENCKEN

+++

There ain't no answer. There ain't gonna be any answer. There never has been an answer. That's the answer.

—GERTRUDE STEIN

++

---

[27] That's right, no one knows.

In diplomacy an ultimatum is the last demand
before concessions.
—AMBROSE BIERCE

✦✦✦

Diplomacy—lying in state.
—OLIVER HERFORD

✦✦

Diplomacy is letting someone else have your way.
—LESTER PEARSON

✦✦✦

A diplomat is a person who can tell you to go to hell in such
a way that you actually look forward to the trip.
—CASKIE STINNETT

✦✦

Diplomacy is the art of saying "Nice doggie" until you can
find a rock.
—WILL ROGERS

✦✦✦

Democracy never lasts long. It soon wasted, exhausts, and
murders itself. There never was a democracy yet that did not
commit suicide.
—JOHN ADAMS

✦✦

Ninety per cent of politicians give the other ten per cent
a bad name.
—HENRY KISSINGER

✦✦

Politicians are people who, when they see the light at the end
of the tunnel, order more tunnel.
—SIR JOHN QUINTON

✦✦✦

Feeling good about government is like looking on the bright
side of any catastrophe. When you quit looking on the
bright side, the catastrophe is still there.
—P. J. O'ROURKE

✦✦

The government is like a baby's alimentary canal, with a
happy appetite at one end and no responsibility at the other.
—RONALD REAGAN

✦✦✦

We live in a world in which politics has replaced philosophy.
—MARTIN L. GROSS

✦✦

There are many men of principle in both parties in America,
but there is no party of principle.
—ALEXIS DE TOCQUEVILLE

✦✦✦

of the United States, all, or any of which Articles, when ratified by three fourths of the

A politician . . . one that would circumvent God.
—WILLIAM SHAKESPEARE

++

A politician needs the ability to foretell what is going to happen tomorrow, next week, next month, and next year. And to have the ability afterwards to explain why it didn't happen.
—WINSTON CHURCHILL

+++

There are two things that are important in politics. The first is money . . . and I can't remember what the other one is.
—F. PAUL WILSON

++

All the people who really know how to run the country are busy driving taxicabs and cutting hair.
—GEORGE BURNS

++

I think that all good, right thinking people in this country are sick and tired of being told that all good, right thinking people in this country are fed up with being told that all good, right thinking people in this country are fed up with being sick and tired. I'm certainly not, and I'm sick and tired of being told that I am.
—MONTY PYTHON

+++

aid Legislatures, to be valid to all intents and purposes, as part of the said Constitution;

Anyone who believes exponential growth can go on forever
in a finite world is either a madman or an economist.
—KENNETH BOULDING

✦✦✦

What this country needs are more unemployed politicians.
—EDWARD LANGLEY

✦✦

American politicians will do anything for money; English
politicians will take the money and won't do anything.
—STEPHEN LEACOCK

✦✦✦

The imbecility of men is always inviting the impudence of
power.
—RALPH WALDO EMERSON

✦✦

I can give you 1040 good reasons why I hate the government.
—TERRI GUILLEMETS

~✦~

*Q: Are we EVER going to have a federal tax
system that regular people can understand?
A: Our top political leaders have all voiced
strong support for this idea.
Q: So you're saying it will never happen?
A: Pretty much.*

~✦~

viz. ✦ ARTICLES in addition to, and Amendment of the Constitution of the Unite

The problem of power is, how to get men of power to live for the public rather than off the public.
—ROBERT F. KENNEDY

٭٭

All political lives, unless they are cut off in midstream at a happy juncture, end in failure, because that is the nature of politics and of human affairs.
—ENOCH POWELL

٭٭٭

The enemy isn't conservatism.
The enemy isn't liberalism. The enemy is bullshit.
—LARS-ERIK NELSON

٭٭

several States, pursuant to the fifth Article of the original Constitution. • Note: T

LIBERALS

llowing text is a transcription of the first ten amendments to the Constitution in their

LIBERALS

It ain't easy bein' a Liberal . . . it's the closest thing the American political system has to sanctioning paranoid schizophrenia. If you're a liberal, you are against capital punishment but firmly believe in a woman's right to choose. You think business is bad but that big government is good. It started out so innocently, mostly used as a term with which one could address a classical education.. "liberal" as in liberty . . . free from constraints of the more rigid aspects of society. Libertine . . . libertarian . . . these monikers invoke a touch of the vitriol when spoken by those of "other" doctrine. But, like most words, it was changed and bastardized and got lost along the way.

Liberals want misery spread equally.

+

Forget the Flag. Burn a Politician.

+

A liberal is a man who is always willing to spend somebody else's money.[28]

+

A liberal is a conservative who hasn't been mugged yet.[29]

+

Question authority before it questions you!

+

Annoy a liberal. Work hard and smile.

---

[28] Carter Glass

[29] Frank Rizzo

I've tried to see it from the liberal point of view, but I can't get my head that far up my ass.

✦

The radical invents the views. When he has worn them out the conservative adopts them.[30]

✦

Grow your own dope! Plant a politician!

✦

A liberal is a conservative who has been arrested.[31]

✦

Want to make liberals angry? Defend the United States.[32]

✦

How do you know a liberal is dead? His heart stops bleeding.

---

[30] Mark Twain
[31] Tom Wolfe

[32] Ann Coulter

an establishment of religion, or prohibiting the free exercise thereof; or abridging th

When a Cigar Isn't a Cigar

We have an awful lot of members who don't understand that
harass is one word, not two.

—PAT SCHROEDER

IMAGINE BEING UNDER A microscope, 24/7. Your
every move is scrutinized, your every tweet parsed, every hotel bill is checked and re-checked, every dime you ever
spent analyzed . . .

Now, imagine the size of the ego one has to have to
ignore all that and screw around, cheat, womanize (and the
female equivalent), double-cross, conspire, collude, contrive,
and more. Hard to get it all in.

Throughout political history, that 1% in the seat of power
has always considered themselves exempt from the rules that
govern the remaining 99% of us.

Sex scandals have plagued the political body from time immemorial. And as can be seen in the previous book on sex[33], nothing brings the snark hammer down every time and rings the bell quite like it.

Yet . . . you want to read all about it, don'tcha?

Nobody believes a rumor here in Washington until it's officially denied.
—EDWARD CHEYFITZ

♦♦

They don't call me Tyrannosaurus Sex for nothing.
—TED KENNEDY

♦♦♦

If everybody in this town connected with politics had to leave town because of chasing women and drinking, you would have no government.
—BARRY GOLDWATER

♦♦

I even accept for the sake of argument that sexual orgies eliminate social tensions and ought to be encouraged.
—SUPREME COURT JUSTICE ANTONIN SCALIA

♦♦♦

---

[33] *The Snark Handbook: Sex Edition*. The art is pretty hot—if I were you, I'd make sure to get a copy.

You think the President of the United States wants to fuck every woman he meets? Well, bad example.
—WOODY ALLEN

~♦~

Newt Gingrich said in an interview this week that the adoption of same-sex marriage in New York showed the nation is "drifting toward a terrible muddle" and that the nation should be defending the federal Defense of Marriage Act, which defines marriage as being between a man and a series of women.

~♦~

Not everyone is happy about the library. Some architectural critics say that the library looks like a doublewide trailer. . . . In fact there is even a sign outside that says: 'If the library is rocking don't come a knocking.'"
—CONAN O'BRIEN, ON THE CLINTON PRESIDENTIAL LIBRARY

♦♦

I know that it's not possible that this child could be mine.
—JOHN EDWARDS

♦♦♦

Name the Politicians Who DIDN'T Father a "Love Child" or Two[34]

A. Grover Cleveland

B. John Edwards

C. Strom Thurmond

D. Ulysses S. Grant

E. Thomas Jefferson

F. Benjamin Franklin

G. Jesse Jackson

H. Franklin D. Roosevelt

~•~

I'd never run for president. I've thought about it, and the only reason I'm not is that I'm scared no woman would come forward and say she had sex with me.

—GARRY SHANDLING

••

In the Clinton administration, we worried the President would open his zipper. In the Bush administration, they worry the President will open his mouth.

—JAMES CARVILLE

•••

Bill Clinton misunderstood the role of the president, which is to screw the country as a whole, not individually.

—BETSY SUSSKIND

••

---

[34] D. (Grant) and H. (Roosevelt). While both had affairs, they must have used protection . . . and we ain't talkin' Secret Service here.

and bear Arms, shall not be infringed. • Amendment III: No Soldier shall, in time c

~•~

The first ladies of the UK, Russia and France were having a meeting with Hilary Clinton. The subject of discussion was the penis of their respective spouse. The first lady of the UK says, "It is like a gentleman—it stands up, as soon as I enter the room". The lady from Russia says, "It is like an army officer- you do not know where he will attack from—front or back." The French lady says, "It is like the curtain in a theatre—once the act is performed, it drops down." Then Hilary says, "It's like a rumor . . . it moves from one mouth to another . . ."

~•~

If you work for Bill Clinton, you go up and down more times than a whore's nightgown.

—JAMES CARVILLE

••

Clinton gets so much action that every couple of weeks they have to spray WD-40 on his zipper.

—DAVID LETTERMAN

•••

Q: What's the difference between a whore and a congressman?

A: A congressman makes more money.

—EDWARD ABBEY

Match the Politician to the Sex Scandal[35]

A. Andrew Jackson	E. Charles Robb
B. Barney Frank	F. Robert Packwood
C. Bob Barr	G. Eric Massa
D. Jim McGreevey	H. Wilbur Mills

~ + ~

1. While married—to President Johnson's daughter, no less—this senator received a nude massage from Miss Virginia. Was there a happy ending?

2. This congressman introduced the "Defense of Marriage" act - and was subsequently photographed licking whipped cream off of strippers at his inaugural party.

3. His diary of sexual exploits really got this senator in trouble when claims of sexual abuse and assault were leveled at him by ten different women.

4. Married a woman presumed to be divorced...who wasn't. Huge scandal that was used against him in the presidential election...some 30 years later.

5. Discovered drunk and beaten up, in the company of an Argentinian stripper, with whom he was having an affair.

6. Appointed his male lover to a position in Homeland Security position. His wife wasn't happy.

---

[35]   1.E., 2. C, 3, E, 4. A., 5. H., 6. D., 7. G, 8.,B.

7. Who said "groping and tickling" weren't just part of a fun work environment? Employees of this congressman.
8. This esteemed congressman had an affair early in his career with a male prostitute who proceeded to service tricks out of his home.

~•~

The two major party presidential candidates today agreed that Americans are seeing too much inappropriate material in popular entertainment.

However, they disagreed on the details . . .

The Republican candidate, George W. Bush, stated that there is too much bloody violence in the movies and on television. Vice President Al Gore, his Democratic opponent, stated meanwhile that the media present Americans with too much sex and frontal nudity.

In other words, Bush says there is too much gore, and Gore says there is too much bush.

~•~

In politics nothing is contemptible.
—BENJAMIN DISRAELI

++

Politics have no relation to morals.
—NICCOLO MACHIAVELLI

~+~

*Hey, stop me if you've heard this one already . . .
A drunk, a sexual harasser, a moron and a flip-
flopper walk into a debate . . . oh, you have? It's
an old joke? Sorry.*

~+~

If presidents don't do it to their wives, they do it the country.
—MEL BROOKS

+++

Too much reading about heterosexual sex.
—BARNEY FRANK ON THE STARR REPORT

++

Women Have Sex Scandals, Too[36]

*Claimed pornographic videos on her expense account. (Jacqui Smith, Home Secretary for the U.K.)

*Nicknamed "The Mattress" for allegedly using sex to get ahead in politics. (Golda Meir, the fourth Prime Minister of Israel)

*Admitted to a six-year affair with a married man who later worked for her congressional staff. (Helen Chenoweth, Republican Congresswoman from Idaho)

*Was videotaped—by her husband, by accident—in bed with someone else. (Katherine Bryson, state representative in Utah)

*Had an affair with a man forty years her junior, earning her the nickname "Celtic Cougar." (Iris Robinson, member of Parliament and wife of the First Minister in Northern Ireland)

*Distributed penis-shaped cookies. (Barbara Cubin, Republican Congresswoman from Wyoming)

*Described sexual exploits with the political elite on her blog, Washingtonienne. (Jessica Cutler, former congressional staff assistant)

*Seduced and married four men, two of whom were her brothers, to maintain political power. (Cleopatra)

---

[36] They just aren't usually caught.

ause, supported by Oath or affirmation, and particularly describing the place to be

What Democratic congressmen do to their women staffers,
Republican congressmen do to the country.
—BILL MAHER

~✦~

*California has passed a law that requires
schools to teach gay history . . . although, those
that disagree with the law are trying to get
around it by interpreting that to mean the story
of the Enola Gay and the novels of Gay Talese.*

~✦~

You know, if I were a single man, I might ask that mummy
out. That's a good-looking mummy.
—BILL CLINTON, REMARKING ABOUT AN INCAN
MUMMY ON DISPLAY AT THE NATIONAL
GEOGRAPHIC MUSEUM

✦✦✦

Match the Senator to His Sex Scandal[37]

A. Mark Sanford   D. David Vitter
B. John Edwards   E. Gary Hart
C. Larry Craig   F. John Ensign

~•~

1. He disappeared after telling his wife he was hiking the Appalachian Trail—which turned out to be another woman in Buenos Ares.
2. Had an affair with a staffer (whose husband also worked for him) that was disclosed at his own Fox News press conference.
3. Ran on a big moral platform until he was caught with a high-priced call girl.
4. Arrested at the Minneapolis airport for disorderly conduct, after playing footsie with another man in an adjoining men's room stall...who turned out to be an undercover agent.
5. Once a VP hopeful, he fell for a filmmaker who he hired to cover his campaign, fathered her child, and used campaign funds to hide it all. The trifecta.
6. "Monkey Business." You remember, the boat, the candidate, the not-his-wife on his lap. 'Nuff said.

---

[37] 1.A.,2.F.,3. D.,4. C, 5. B., 6. E.

eld to answer for a capital, or otherwise infamous crime, unless on a presentment or

~+~

_____ (insert politician's name here), distraught over his latest sexual indiscretion, was walking the grounds looking for any kind of guidance. He goes first to the Washington Monument, looks up and says, "George, you were always wise, what should I do?" Low and behold, a voice comes down from above and says, "ABOLISH THE I.R.S. AND START OVER."

Amazed that he is talking to the past, the politician thinks he'll try it again. He walks over to the Jefferson Memorial and utters the same request to America's author of the Declaration of Independence and one of its great early philosophers. "Thomas, you never had these kind of problems, what can I do to rally people behind me?" Again a voice from above answers, "WELFARE, IT'S NOT WORKING, ABOLISH IT, START OVER."

After hearing this, he is so excited he decides to go to all the historic sites for guidance. Next he goes to the Lincoln Memorial for advice from the President who met his untimely death after winning the Civil War and keeping the country unified. "Abe, I need your help. People are losing confidence in me and they no longer trust me. What should I do?" After a substantial pause Abe responds, "TAKE THE DAY OFF, GO TO THE THEATER."

~+~

In government, a "highly placed source" is the person who started the rumor.
—SAM EWING

++

If you want to succeed in politics you must keep your conscience firmly under control.
—DAVID LLOYD GEORGE

+++

In Washington, we know there's a huge difference between a prostitute and a politician. There are some things a prostitute won't do.
—SEN. CLAIRE MCCASKILL

ilitia, when in actual service in time of War or public danger; nor shall any person

Hello? Do Not. Tweet. Text. Email. Your Sex.

1. Rep. Anthony Weiner - Serial tweeter who sent lewd pix of his genitalia to at least six young women around the country...then claimed it was a hacker... until it was conclusively proven otherwise.
2. Mark Foley - Sent sexually explicit messages to a young man. Has yet to publish his book of poetry.
3. Mayor Kwame Kilpatrick - Had an affair with a city official, discovered by the Detroit free Press in a lengthy series of text messages.
4. Eliot Spitzer - The former New York governor forced to resign after the Feds tracked text messages from a madame called "Rachelle" to a prostitute called "Kristen.
5. Joe Stagni - City Councilman from small town in Louisiana, admitted he sent a snap of himself in his undies to a city employee, but only after the image showed up on the city computer server.
6. Louis N. Magazzu - A New Jersey County commissioner. Began a cyber-affair as his marriage fell apart and never met his amour. Just another "My Dong, My Resignation" scandal.

7. Christopher Lee - Sent flirtatious e-mails and a shirtless photo in response to a personal ad of a single 34-year-old woman on Craigslist.
8. James E. West - Removed as mayor of Spokane, WA, after an gay Internet sex scandal.

liberty, or property, without due process of law; nor shall private property be taken fo

I Am Not a Crook

There is no distinctly American criminal class—except
Congress.
—MARK TWAIN

THERE'S HARDLY A DAY that goes by in these
times when the 24/7 news media isn't breaking in
with a story of some politician, somewhere, doing something
wrong. Between sexual indiscretion, illegal power-monger-
ing, improper funding, more sexual malarkey (Footnote—
are these people stupid enough to believe the Internet is
anonymous?), corruption, bribery, cronyism, even MORE
sexual misbehavior, nepotism, patronage, graft . . . the list
could go on forever. And that's not counting them humding-
ers like treason and sedition.

Weirdly enough, many think that this is a relatively new
phenomenon that started with Nixon and trickled down
through today. Not so, oh naïve one. Politicians have been
playing fast and loose with the law since the beginning of

government. From Jefferson's out-of–wedlock child with Sally Hemming to the carpetbaggers of the Civil War, the adage that "Power corrupts but absolute power corrupts absolutely" holds sway throughout history.

It's been the stuff of movies and books forever. And, of course, myriads have snarked about it. Here's some of the best.

I haven't committed a crime. What I did was fail to comply with the law.
—DAVID DINKINS

++

We hang the petty thieves and appoint the great ones to public office.
—AESOP

+++

I was really too honest a man to be a politician and live.
—SOCRATES

++

Believe nothing until it has been officially denied.
—CLAUDE COCKBURN

+++

Rutherford B. Hayes: His Fraudulency.
—ANON

✦✦✦

He is such an infernal liar.
—ULYSSES S. GRANT [ON ANDREW JOHNSON]

✦✦

Filthy storyteller, despot, liar, thief, braggart, buffoon,
usurper, monster, ignoramus Abe, old scoundrel, perjurer,
swindler, tyrant, field-butcher,
land-pirate . . .
—HARPERS MAGAZINE [ON ABRAHAM LINCOLN]

✦✦✦

Turnacoat Tyler.
—POPULAR SLOGAN OF THE DAY [ABOUT JOHN TYLER]

✦✦

I would have made a good Pope!
—RICHARD M. NIXON

✦✦✦

There are a lot of people who lie and get away with it,
and that's just a fact.
—DONALD RUMSFELD

✦✦

He is ignorant, passionate, hypocritical, corrupt and easily
swayed by the basest men who surround him.
—HENRY CLAY [ON ANDREW JACKSON]

+++

In Louisiana we don't bet on football games, we bet on
whether a politician is going to be indicted or not.
—MARK DUFFY

++

I would not like to be a political leader in Russia. They never
know when they're being taped.
—RICHARD NIXON

+++

If one morning I walked on top of the water across the
Potomac River, the headline that afternoon would read:
'President Can't Swim.'
—LYNDON JOHNSON

++

If I were two-faced, would I be wearing this one?
—ABRAHAM LINCOLN

+++

Over the years the quality of our presidential timber has declined; today we are pretty much satisfied if our president stays out of jail and occasionally emits a complete sentence.

—DAVE BARRY

✦✦✦

Crime does not pay . . . as well as politics.

—ALFRED E. NEWMAN

✦✦✦

One way to make sure crime doesn't pay would be to let the government run it.

—RONALD REAGAN

✦✦

Politicians are wedded to the truth, but unlike many other married couples they sometimes live apart.

—SAKI

✦✦✦

A good politician is quite as unthinkable as an honest burglar.

—H. L. MENCKEN

✦✦

I have certain rules I live by. My first rule: I don't believe anything the government tells me.

—GEORGE CARLIN

✦✦✦

It's useless to hold anyone to anything he says while he's in love, drunk, or running for office.

—SHIRLEY MACLAINE

~✦~

Q: How long does a Congressman serve?
A: Depends on his sentence.

~✦~

Instead of giving a politician the keys to the city, it might be better to change the locks.

—DOUG LARSON

✦✦

The cardinal rule of politics—never get caught in bed with a live man or a dead woman.

—J. R. EWING

✦✦✦

When a politician changes his position it's sometimes hard to tell whether he has seen the light or felt the heat.

—ROBERT FUOS

✦✦

WHAT $50,000 WILL BUY YOU IN WASHINGTON, DC[38]

↪ 2 First Class tickets to Cabo, luggage included

↪ 2 seats in the Senate

↪ 4 seats in the House

↪ 6 seats at a Bruce Springsteen concert (first 10 rows)

↪ 3,547 "World's Best Lobbyist" mugs

↪ A 2:00 P.M. Tee Time at St. Andrews

↪ Half of a diamond encrusted thong

↪ Skybox tickets at any arena in America

↪ A life-size replica of yourself in Lego blocks

↪ Your own war

↪ Vegas, baby

The infectiousness of crime is like that of the plague.
—NAPOLEON BONAPARTE

++

[38] With the right lobbyist

In a closed society where everybody's guilty, the only crime is getting caught. In a world of thieves, the only final sin is stupidity.

—HUNTER S. THOMPSON

✦✦✦

The only power any government has is the power to crack down on criminals. Well, when there aren't enough criminals, one makes them. One declares so many things to be a crime that it becomes impossible for men to live without breaking laws.

—AYN RAND

✦✦

Organized crime in America takes in over forty billion dollars a year and spends very little on office supplies.

—WOODY ALLEN

✦✦✦

Homosexuality in Russia is a crime and the punishment is seven years in prison, locked up with the other men. There is a three year waiting list.

—YAKOV SMIRNOFF

✦✦

Nixon told us he was going to take crime out of the streets. He did. He took it into the damn White House.

—RALPH ABERNATHY

✦✦✦

A politician can appear to have his nose to the grindstone while straddling a fence and keeping both ears to the ground.

—ANON

++

The reason there are so few female politicians is that it is too much trouble to put makeup on two faces.

—MAUREEN MURPHY

+++

As a rule of thumb, if the government wants you to know it, it probably isn't true.

—CRAIG MURRAY

++

Democracy is defended in 3 stages. Ballot Box, Jury Box, Cartridge Box.

—AMBROSE BIERCE

+++

Bureaucracy defends the status quo long past the time when the quo has lost its status.

—LAURENCE J. PETER

++

The illegal we do immediately. The unconstitutional takes
a little longer.
—HENRY KISSINGER

+++

The truth is a frequent casualty in the heat of an election
campaign.
—TIP O'NEILL

++

Avoid all needle drugs. The only dope worth shooting is
Richard Nixon.
—ABBIE HOFFMAN

+++

Nixon impeached himself. He gave us Gerald Ford as his revenge.
—BELLA ABZUG

++

He is a man of his most recent word.
—WILLIAM F. BUCKLEY [ON LYNDON JOHNSON]

+++

No man's life, liberty, or property is safe while the
legislature is in session.
—MARK TWAIN

++

When you start looking for some politician's footprints on
the sands of time, steer for the mud holes first.
—ROBERT ELLIOT GONZALES

+++

Politics: the art of appearing candid and completely open
while concealing as much as possible.
—FRANK HERBERT, IN *DUNE*

✦✦

Political language. . . is designed to make lies sound truthful
and murder respectable.
—GEORGE ORWELL

✦✦✦

People always ask me, "where were you when Kennedy got
shot?" . . . Well, I don't have an alibi.
—EMO PHILIPS

✦✦

If a politician murders his mother, the first response of
the press or of his opponents will likely be not that it was
a terrible thing to do, but rather that in a statement made
six years before he had gone on record as being opposed to
matricide.
—MEG GREENFIELD

✦✦✦

There is no kind of dishonesty into which otherwise
good people more easily and frequently fall than that of
defrauding the government.
—BENJAMIN FRANKLIN

✦✦

Whenever a man has cast a longing eye on offices, a rottenness begins in his conduct.
—THOMAS JEFFERSON

✦✦✦

Son, if you can't take their money, drink their whiskey, screw their women, and then vote against 'em, you don't deserve to be here.
—SAM RAYBURN, FORMER SPEAKER OF THE HOUSE

✦✦

When the President does it, it means it's not illegal.
—RICHARD NIXON

✦✦✦

Washington, DC is to lying what Wisconsin is to cheese.
—DENNIS MILLER

✦✦

I don't care who does the electing just so long as I do the nominating.
—WILLIAM "BOSS" TWEED[39]

✦✦✦

It is hard to believe that a man is telling the truth when you know that you would lie if you were in his place.
—H. L. MENCKEN

✦✦

---

[39] The most corrupt American politician of the 19th century

'Reform' is a word you always oughta' watch out for. 'Reform'
is a change that you're supposed to like. And watch it—as
soon as you hear the word 'Reform', you [should] reach for
your wallet and see who's lifting it.

—NOAM CHOMSKY

+++

People demand freedom of speech as a compensation for the
freedom of thought, which they never use.

—SOREN AABYE KIERKEGAARD

++

If they can get you asking the wrong questions, they don't
have to worry about the answers.

—THOMAS PYNCHON

+++

I either want less corruption, or more chance to participate
in it.

—ASHLEIGH BRILLIANT

++

I'm spending a year dead for tax reasons.

—DOUGLAS ADAMS

+++

When they call the roll in the Senate, the Senators do not
know whether to answer 'present' or 'not guilty.

—TEDDY ROOSEVELT

++

X: The powers not delegated to the United States by the Constitution, nor prohibite

CONSERVATIVES

CONSERVATIVES

It ain't easy bein' a Conservative. You have to walk that nearly undetectable line that runs exactly down the middle. You have to maintain the traditional so vehemently that it can make your head spin. And all the while that you're keeping any and all change at the absolute minimal allowable, you are also trying, ever so diligently, to persuade the world that GRADUAL change in society is necessary. Like I said . . . not so easy. Take a look.

Liberals feel unworthy of their possessions. Conservatives feel they deserve everything they've stolen.[40]

+

A conservative is too cowardly to fight and too fat to run.[41]

+

A conservative is someone who believes in reform. But not now.[42]

+

Proud member of the vast right-wing conspiracy

---

[40] Mort Sahl   [41] Elbert Hubbard   [42] Mort Sahl

May the fetus you save be gay

•

Churches should stay out of politics or be taxed.

•

A conservative is a man who just sits and thinks, mostly sits.[43]

•

The Christian Right is neither.[44]

•

Conservatives define them-selves in terms of what they oppose.[45]

•

Right is right and wrong is wrong, no matter what the spin.

•

Evolution is a theory . . . kind of like gravity

•

I'd rather be waterboarding.[46]

---

43 Woodrow Wilson

44 Moby

45 George Will

46 Conservative bumper sticker

War and Other Ways to Make a Statement

When in doubt, start a war.
—BUMPER STICKER

YESIREEBOBCATTAIL . . . IF YOUR numbers start to slip . . . if the American people start to turn . . . when the economy's in the crapper . . . or you need to get a bunch of folks hired quick . . . start a war.

There's precedent. FDR led us into World War II. Truman finished that one and started one in Korea. John F. Kennedy began Vietnam in 1962 and Johnson ratcheted it up a tad. Clinton had Bosnia, Somalia, and Kosovo. And Bush has at least two and a half on his tally sheet. It definitely makes a statement. But be careful . . . someone just might have somethin' to say about it.

War, n: A time-tested political tactic guaranteed to raise a president's popularity rating by at least 30 points. It is especially useful during election years and economic downturns.

—CHAZ BUFE

♦♦

The reason the American Army does so well in wartime, is that war is chaos, and the American Army practices it on a daily basis.

—GERMAN GENERAL

♦♦♦

Anything worth fighting for is worth fighting dirty for.

—ANON

♦♦

I haven't heard the president state that we're at war. That's why I too do not know—do we use the term intervention? Do we use war? Do we use squirmish? What is it?"

—SARAH PALIN, ON LIBYA

♦♦♦

REAR, n. In American military matters, that exposed part of the army that is nearest to Congress.

—AMBROSE BIERCE

♦♦

War makes rattling good history; but peace is poor reading.

—THOMAS HARDY

♦♦♦

We have women in the military, but they don't put us in the front lines. They don't know if we can fight, if we can kill. I think we can. All the general has to do is walk over to the women and say, 'You see the enemy over there? They say you look fat in those uniforms.'"

—ELAYNE BOOSLER

✦✦✦

It will be a great day when our schools have all the money they need, and our air force has to have a bake-sale to buy a bomber.

—ROBERT FULGHUM

✦✦

We, the willing, led by the unknowing, are doing the impossible for the ungrateful. We have now done so much for so long with so little, we are now capable of doing anything with nothing.

—ANON

✦✦✦

We are not retreating—we are advancing in another direction.

—GENERAL DOUGLAS MACARTHUR

✦✦

You really can't blame the military for wanting to go to war [in Iraq]. They've got all these new toys and they want to know whether they work or not.

—ANDY ROONEY

✦✦✦

commenced or prosecuted against one of the United States by Citizens of another State,

Before a war, military science seems a real science, like astronomy; but after a war, it seems more like astrology.
—REBECCA WEST

✦✦

The Army has carried the American . . . ideal to its logical conclusion. Not only do they prohibit discrimination on the grounds of race, creed and color, but also on ability.
—TOM LEHRER

✦✦✦

We have twelve thousand troops. But that's not enough. That's the amount that is going to die. And at the end of a war you need some soldiers left, really, or else it looks like you've lost.
—GENERAL GEORGE MILLER FROM *IN THE LOOP*

✦✦

Make the lie big, make it simple, keep saying it, and eventually they will believe it.
—ADOLPH HITLER

✦✦✦

I only know two tunes: One of them is "Yankee Doodle" and the other isn't.
—ULYSSES S. GRANT

✦✦

Match the President to His War[47]

A. George Washington   F. Woodrow Wilson

B. James Madison   G. Franklin D. Roosevelt

C. James Monroe   H. Harry Truman

D. James Polk   I. George H. Bush

E. William McKinley   J. George W. Bush

~+~

1. The Revolutionary War (1775-1783)
2. Iraqi Invasion and Occupation (2003...)
3. World War II (1939-1945)
4. War of 1812
5. Korean War (1950-1953)
6. Persian Gulf War I with Iraq (1990)
7. World War I (1914-1918)
8. Spanish-American War (1898)
9. Mexican War (1846-1848)
10. Indian Wars of 1817

---

[47] I.A., 2.J., 3.G., 4.B., 5.H., 6.I., 7.F., 8. E., 9.D., 10.C.

O peace! How many wars were waged in thy name?
—ALEXANDER POPE

✦✦

A great war leaves a country with three armies: an army of cripples, an army of mourners, and an army of thieves.
—ANONYMOUS

✦✦✦

The world cannot continue to wage war like physical giants and to seek peace like intellectual pygmies.
—BASIL O'CONNOR

✦✦

If this were a dictatorship, it'd be a heck of a lot easier, just so long as I'm the dictator.
—GEORGE W. BUSH

✦✦✦

"My country right or wrong" is like saying, "My mother drunk or sober."
—G. K. CHESTERTON

✦✦

Military justice is to justice what military music is to music.
—GROUCHO MARX

✦✦✦

A visitor from Mars could easily pick out the civilized nations. They have the best implements of war.
—HERBERT PROCHNOW

✦✦

The object of war is not to die for your country but to make
the other bastard die for his.
—GENERAL GEORGE PATTON

✦✦✦

My hope is that gays will be running the world, because then
there would be no war. Just a greater emphasis on military
apparel.
—ROSEANNE BARR

✦✦

A prisoner of war is a man who tries to kill you and fails,
and then asks you not to kill him.
—WINSTON CHURCHILL

✦✦✦

Nothing is so admirable in politics as a short memory.
—JOHN KENNETH GALBRAITH

✦✦

Pentagon records show that at least 8,000 members of the
all-volunteer U.S. Army have deserted since the Iraq war
began. Hey, at least somebody has an exit strategy.
—TINA FEY

✦✦✦

Asking an incumbent member of Congress to vote for
term limits is a bit like asking a chicken to vote for Colonel
Sanders.
—BOB INGLIS

✦✦

heir respective states and vote by ballot for President and Vice-President, one of whom,

Sen. Hillary Clinton called for President Bush to begin
pulling troops out of Iraq next year. And let me tell you
something, when it comes to telling a president when to pull
out, no one has more experience than Hillary Clinton.

—JAY LENO

✦✦

Military intelligence is a contradiction in terms.

—GROUCHO MARX

~✦~

*George Bush started an ill-timed and disastrous
war under false pretenses by lying to the American people and to the Congress; he ran a budget
surplus into a severe deficit; he consistently and
unconscionably favored the wealthy and corporations over the rights and needs of the population; he destroyed trust and confidence in, and
good will toward, the United States around the
globe; he ignored global warming, to the world's
detriment; he wantonly broke our treaty obli-
gations; he condoned torture of prisoners; he
attempted to create a theocracy in the United
States and appointed incompetent cronies to
positions of vital national importance.*

*So, why didn't someone just give him a
blowjob so we could impeach him?*

~✦~

at least, shall not be an inhabitant of the same state with themselves; they shall name in

Why does the Air Force need expensive new bombers?
Have the people we've been bombing over the years been
complaining?
—GEORGE WALLACE

+++

We do know of certain knowledge that he [Osama Bin
Laden] is either in Afghanistan, or in some other country, or
dead.
—DONALD RUMSFELD (IN 2003)

++

The only way to reduce the number of nuclear weapons is to
use them.
—RUSH LIMBAUGH

+++

Government is the Entertainment division of the military-
industrial complex.
—FRANK ZAPPA

++

The Homeland Security System. They had it color-coded,
like we're in elementary school. Simplify it, there should be
just three levels of security: Jesus Christ, Goddammit and
FUCK ME!
—LEWIS BLACK

+++

All war is deception.
—SUN TZU

++

"War . . . What is it good for? Absolutely nothing."
—EDWIN STARR

+++

We found the term 'killing' too broad.
—STATE DEPARTMENT SPOKESPERSON ON WHY THE
WORD 'KILLING' WAS REPLACED WITH 'UNLAWFUL OR
ARBITRARY DEPRIVATION OF LIFE'.

++

From a marketing point of view, you don't roll out new
products in August.
—WHITE HOUSE CHIEF OF STAFF ANDREW CARD, ON
WHY THE BUSH ADMINISTRATION WAITED UNTIL
AFTER LABOR DAY TO TRY TO SELL THE AMERICAN
PEOPLE ON WAR AGAINST IRAQ.

+++

War is God's way of teaching Americans geography.
—AMBROSE BIERCE

++

Sixty years ago Hitler invaded Poland. This led to the
creation of The History Channel.
—JAY LENO

+++

I detest war; it ruins conversation.
—BERNARD FONTENELLE

++

The Gulf War was like teenage sex. We got in too
soon and out too soon.
—TOM HARKIN

+++

In times of disorder and stress, the fanatics play a prominent
role; in times of peace, the critics. Both are shot after the
revolution.
—EDMUND WILSON

++

A patriot must always be ready to defend his country against
his government.
—EDWARD ABBEY

+++

lists they shall sign and certify, and transmit sealed to the seat of the government of th

Lowest Common Denominator

"**D**O NOT ARGUE WITH an idiot. He will drag you down to his level and beat you with experience."

I open this chapter with a well-known joke, as it brilliantly summarizes much of the governmental imbeciles we know and mock.

When did it happen? When did being smart cease to be a requirement for running for office? When did the ability to string multi-syllabic words together to form sentences come to mean elitist and the phrase " he's an intellectual" become a pejorative? When did the "dumbing down" of America hit the Capital? Some say time immemorial . . . it's getting hard to argue.

As I started to research the many faux pas, blunders and moronic misstatements that characterize many of the political wannabe's that have come down the proverbial pike over the last few decades, I was overwhelmed by the sheer abundance of material to choose from . . . these past few years in particular.

Have a look . . . but not too long . . . your brain may turn to stone.

One word sums up probably the responsibility of any vice president, and that one word is 'to be prepared.'[48]
—AL GORE

+++

Washington is a Hollywood for ugly people. Hollywood is a Washington for the simpleminded.
—JOHN MCCAIN

++

They're our next-door neighbors and you can actually see Russia from land here in Alaska, from an island in Alaska.
—SARAH PALIN

+++

You know, education—if you make the most of it—you study hard, you do your homework and you make an effort to be smart, you can do well. If you don't, you get stuck in Iraq.
—JOHN KERRY

++

---

[48] Also attributed to Dan Quayle

The Day After Osama bin Laden Was Killed ...

Sarah Palin said, "I knew he was dead because I watched the whole thing from my porch".

++

Donald Trump asked to see his death certificate.

+++

Mitt Romney filled out an application at Starbucks.

++

The Pakistani Government said, " Oh, THAT Osama ... "

+++

Geraldo Rivera bought a wet suit.

++

John Boehner cried.

I have left orders to be awakened at any time in case of national emergency—even if I'm in a Cabinet meeting.
—RONALD REAGAN

+++

If we took away the minimum wage—if conceivably it was gone—we could potentially virtually wipe out unemployment completely because we would be able to offer jobs at whatever level.
—MICHELLE BACHMAN

++

What right does Congress have to go around making laws
just because they deem it necessary?'
—MARION BARRY, FORMER MAYOR OF WASHINGTON

~•~

*Donald Trump says he is "proud of himself"
for getting President Obama to release his full
birth certificate. Yep, Don, real good job . . .
got him to take time out from the economy and
jobs, world peace, Iran and Iraq, Immigration,
Health Care, Global Warming, Education,
Taxes . . . and focus on showing the country
a piece of paper we all knew he had anyway
. . . not to mention they cut in and interrupted
Martha Stewart . . .*

~•~

I think that gay marriage should be between a man and a
woman.
—GOV. ARNOLD SCHWARZENEGGER

••

I've noticed that everyone who is for abortion has already
been born.
—RONALD REAGAN

•••

for President, shall be the President, if such number be a majority of the whole numbe

I've now been in 57 states—I think I have one left to go.
—BARACK OBAMA

••

Facts are stupid things.
—RONALD REAGAN, ATTEMPTING TO QUOTE JOHN
ADAMS, WHO SAID, "FACTS ARE STUBBORN THINGS."

•••

I am a man of limited talents from a small town. I don't seem
to grasp that I am the President.
—WARREN G. HARDING

••

Most people would sooner die than think; in fact,
they do so.
—BERTRAND RUSSELL

•••

Obama's got a health care logo that's right out of Adolf
Hitler's playbook . . . Adolf Hitler, like Barack Obama, also
ruled by dictate.
—RUSH LIMBAUGH

••

It may be tempting and more comfortable to just keep your
head down, plod along, and appease those who demand: 'Sit
down and shut up,' but that's the worthless, easy path; that's
a quitter's way out.
—SARAH PALIN, QUITTING HER JOB AS GOVERNOR

•••

of Electors appointed; and if no person have such majority, then from the persons having

Thoughts on Stupidity

Being in politics is like being a football coach. You have to be smart enough to understand the game, and dumb enough to think it's important.
—EUGENE MCCARTHY

++

In politics, stupidity is not a handicap.
—NAPOLEON BONAPARTE

+++

Today's public figures can no longer write their own speeches or books, and there is some evidence that they can't read them either.
—GORE VIDAL

++

I remain just one thing, and one thing only, and that is a clown. It places me on a far higher plane than any politician.
—CHARLIE CHAPLIN

+++

The kind of man who wants the government to adopt and enforce his ideas is always the kind of man whose ideas are idiotic.
—H. L. MENCKEN

++

We need a president who's fluent in at least one language.
—BUCK HENRY

the highest numbers not exceeding three on the list of those voted for as President,

I wouldn't go anywhere in confined places now. . . . When one person sneezes it goes all the way through the aircraft. That's me. I would not be, at this point, if they had another way of transportation, suggesting they ride the subway.
—VICE PRESIDENT BIDEN ABOUT SWINE FLU

++

We need to up tick our image with everyone, including one-armed midgets.
—REPUBLICAN NATIONAL COMMITTEE CHAIRMAN MICHAEL STEELE

~+~

The Freedom of Information Act has forced the state of Alaska to release 24,000 of Sarah Palin's emails from her time as governor. Most telling is the one she sent John McCain when informed she would be his running mate. "This must be the kind of excitement you felt when we won the war in Vietnam, John!"

~+~

George Bush did an incredible job during his presidency, defending us from freedom.
—RICK PERRY

+++

You cannot be president of the United States if you don't have faith. Remember Lincoln, going to his knees in times of trial and the Civil War and all that stuff. You can't be. And we are blessed. So don't feel sorry for—don't cry for me, Argentina. Message: I care.

—GEORGE H.W. BUSH

++

Dan Quayle—King of the Hill

↔ If we don't succeed, we run the risk of failure.

↔ Republicans understand the importance of bondage between a mother and child.

↔ What a waste it is to lose one's mind. Or not to have a mind is being very wasteful. How true that is.

↔ One word sums up probably the responsibility of any vice president, and that one word is 'to be prepared.'[49]

↔ Mars is essentially in the same orbit . . . Mars is somewhat the same distance from the Sun, which is very important. We have seen pictures where there are canals, we believe, and water. If there is water, that means there is oxygen. If oxygen, that means we can breathe.

---

[49] Also attributed to Al Gore

↝ The Holocaust was an obscene period in our nation's history. I mean in this century's history. But we all lived in this century. I didn't live in this century.

↝ There are lots more people in the House. I don't know exactly—I've never counted, but at least a couple hundred.

↝ I believe we are on an irreversible trend toward more freedom and democracy—but that could change.

↝ I love California, I practically grew up in Phoenix.

↝ I was recently on a tour of Latin America, and the only regret I have was that I didn't study Latin harder in school so I could converse with those people.

I just know he has the smallest penis. I mean, we're talking freezing cold acorn in his pants, screaming for cover.
—CARRIE FISHER ON DAN QUAYLE

✦✦✦

Dan Quayle is more stupid than Ronald Reagan put together.
—MATT GROENING

✦✦

I'm against political jokes. Too often they get elected to office.
—HENNY YOUNGMAN

✦✦✦

Marge, the reason we have elected officials is so we don't
have to think!
—HOMER SIMPSON

~✦~

*When politicians moan that America is
"becoming a banana republic," they sometimes get lost in the rhetoric and continue
with, "Hopefully, we will be closing The Gap
between the rich and the poor at OWS and we
won't have to call out The Old Navy so that
this country can finally go to Bed, Bath and
Beyond."*

~✦~

Once upon a time there was a politician who made an
especially conspicuous ass of himself and didn't say the
newspapers misquoted him.
—ROBERT ELLIOT GONZALES

✦✦

from two-thirds of the states, and a majority of all the states shall be necessary to a

"Be excited. This is Joementum here in New Hampshire."
—SEN. JOSEPH LIEBERMAN TO WOLF BLITZER, ON HIS
MOMENTUM LEADING UP TO THE NEW HAMPSHIRE
PRIMARY, WHERE HE CHARACTERIZED HIS FIFTH PLACE
FINISH AS A "THREE-WAY SPLIT DECISION FOR THIRD PLACE."

✦✦✦

The majority is never right. Never, I tell you! That's one of
these lies in society that no free and intelligent man can help
rebelling against. Who are the people that make up the biggest
proportion of the population—the intelligent ones or the fools?
—HENRIK IBSEN, AN ENEMY OF THE PEOPLE

~✦~

*Imagine her surprise when Oakland Mayor
Jean Quan found out her husband had been
working closely with the "Occupy Oakland"
protesters that she had been at war with for
weeks. He is now deeply involved with the
"Occupy The Spare Bedroom" movement.*

~✦~

No one you'd really like to see in public office has the bad
taste to run.
—F. PAUL WILSON

✦✦

choice. [And if the House of Representatives shall not choose a President whenever

CONGRESSIONAL EXCUSES FOR NEVER GETTING ANYTHING DONE

↔ There was massive traffic jam this morning on the way here.

↔ My vote is in the shop.

↔ I couldn't find parking.

↔ I couldn't find my car keys.

↔ I lost my wallet this morning and couldn't leave home without it.

↔ I was mugged coming in today.

↔ I have a Doctor's note to leave early that requires me to do less work around here.

↔ I feel ill and should go home early today.

↔ I have [insert disease here] and won't be able to come in to work for a couple of days.

↔ Sorry I'm late,...I'm moving into a new place.

↔ The power went out last night.

↔ I got food poisoning and won't be able to come in.

↔ What? I didn't know I couldn't do that. Sorry, won't happen again.

↔ I was in the restroom, that's why you couldn't find me. No, not that restroom, the one on the 2nd floor.

↔ I was on a break.

↔ I don't recall that being one of the required skills!

↔ I never got the memo. And {Insert Speaker of House's name} didn't tell me about it.

↔ I really didn't have any clean clothes.

↔ This may sound like a lame excuse, but my dog ate the bill I was working on. No, really, you have to believe me.

↔ [Insert President's name here] told me it was okay to do it.

↔ I was just too drunk to wake up.

I have a wide stance.
—SEN. LARRY CRAIG

✦✦✦

A learned blockhead is a greater blockhead than an ignorant
one.
—BENJAMIN FRANKLIN

✦✦✦

An election? That's one of those deals where they close the
bars isn't it?
—BARNEY GUMBEL

✦✦

The vote on a bill to legalize bisexuality could go either way.
—ANONYMOUS

✦✦✦

See, Barack's been talking down to black people on this
faith-based . . . I want to cut his nuts off.
—JESSE JACKSON

✦✦

They misunderestimate me.
—GEORGE W. BUSH

✦✦✦

I'm just not giving it up for f***in' nothing. I'm not gonna do
it. And, and I can always use it. I can parachute me there.
. . . Give this motherf****r Obama his senator? F**k him.
For nothing. F**k him.
—ILLINOIS GOV. ROD BLAGOJEVICH

✦✦

I was under medication when I made the decision to burn
the tapes.
—RICHARD NIXON

♦♦

We need to execute people like John Walker Lindh in order
to physically intimidate liberals.
—ANN COULTER

♦♦♦

You cannot go to a 7-11 or a Dunkin' Donuts unless you
have a slight Indian accent.
—JOE BIDEN

♦♦

Considering the dire circumstances that we have in New
Orleans, virtually a city that has been destroyed, things are
going relatively well.
—FEMA DIRECTOR MICHAEL BROWN

♦♦♦

I know how hard it is for you to put food on your family.
—GEORGE W. BUSH

♦♦

otes as Vice-President, shall be the Vice-President, if such number be a majority of the

~•~

These GOP debaters do love them some oligarchy. Newt Gingrich, arguing about Social Security, cited a model favored by Chile that was conceptualized under Allende and forced upon the citizenry by Pinochet. Hey, maybe we should bring back the Caravan of Death? Armed with pepper spray, perhaps? What say ye, Blitz?

~•~

Do you know, where does this phrase 'separation of church and state' come from? It was not in Jefferson's letter to the Danbury Baptists. . . . The exact phrase 'separation of Church and State' came out of Adolph Hitler's mouth, that's where it comes from. So the next time your liberal friends talk about the separation of Church and State, ask them why they're Nazis.

—GLEN URQUHART

••

They want the federal government controlling Social Security like it's some kind of federal program.

—GEORGE W. BUSH

•••

Things are more like they are now than they have ever been.
—PRESIDENT GERALD FORD

✦✦

China is a big country, inhabited by many Chinese.
—CHARLES DE GAULLE, EX-FRENCH PRESIDENT

✦✦✦

This is a great day for France!
—PRESIDENT RICHARD NIXON WHILE ATTENDING
CHARLES DE GAULLE'S FUNERAL.

✦✦

We are ready for any unforeseen event that may or may not
occur.
—VICE PRESIDENT AL GORE

✦✦✦

the purpose shall consist of two-thirds of the whole number of Senators, and a majority

Conclusion

We've seen . . . an evolution from one propertied man, one vote; to one man, one vote; to one person, one vote; trending to one dollar, one vote.

—MICHAEL SPENCE, NOBEL PRIZE-WINNING ECONOMIST

OUCH! CLEARLY, THERE'S ONLY one way to deal with what we have in front of us: Snark.

"Foul!" you may cry. "It's too easy to be cynical, to be cavalier, to be distrustful or doubtful or jaded or . . . well, snarky." I'm here to tell you that easy or not, that's the only way to survive the incessantly ridiculous proposals put forth by our government, by politicians, by, let's face it, the corporations that actually seem to run the United States of America.

Yes, the system may be fucked beyond all possible repairs. Yes, the system may be rife with corruption and depravity and immorality and, quite possibly, evil . . . Yes, it seems like it is far too big to change and all we can do is to try to defend ourselves to the best of our abilities.

It's all true. But can you just give up? Call it a day? Throw in the towel?

Hey, if the government can invade a country because "intelligence" told them that there might be some weapons of mass destruction; if a bunch of angry jobless people can occupy a park and say it's Wall Street—and become liberal media darlings in the process . . . I think the country is up for anything. Including a massive infusion of snark.

Snark loud and snark often. Snark long and snark hard. Learn from the wise words contained in this book while you have it in your hot little hands. (After all, *The Snark Handbook* could be banned someday.[50])

If all else fails, remember: Vote early and vote often.

And for the love of America, stay snarky.

---

[50] Or used as a torture device now that waterboarding is off the table.

ineligible to the office of President shall be eligible to that of Vice-President of the

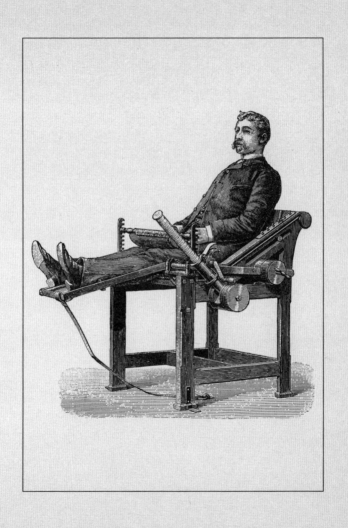

I, section 4, of the Constitution was modified by section 2 of this amendment.

Acknowledgments

To my amazing editor, Ann—moderate with the pen, conservative with her snark, but always liberal with her praise;

To my usual gang of cronies and cohorts, snarky to the bitter end.

And, as always, to RP, who governs my heart.